LEAD ME, REALLY!

Transforming Heart & Mind to Produce...

Authentic Leadership

JOSÉ A. LUGOSANTIAGO

WAJ-BOOK PRESS

Lead Me, Really! Transforming Heart & Mind to Produce Authentic Leadership

José A. LugoSantiago

Published in the U.S.A by WAJ-Book Press, San Antonio, Texas.

Paperback Version: ISBN 978-0-9904990-4-6

Electronic Version: ISBN 978-0-9904990-5-3

Library of Congress Control Number: 2016911307

For information about special discounts for bulk purchases, or leadership training, please contact us at

wajbookpress@eassistantww.com.

Printed by CreateSpace, a DBA of On-Demand Publishing, LLC.

The views expressed in this book are solely those of the author.

Contents

———

Acknowledgments

————

To you who cares for another, who's not afraid to guide the blind, and who strives to be stronger, the supreme servant and real leader. Your passion encourages me. This book is for you, the real leader. I hope this work elevates the caliber of your leadership from the inside so that it can flow outward.

To the friends who became my family and to my natural family (wife, sons, parents, sister, aunts, uncles, cousins, nephews), I think about all of you often. You are an inspiration of love, my memory of how happy we all can be. Even when it appeared we didn't have much, we had everything.

To the thousands of Airmen, Soldiers, Marines, Sailors, Coastguardsmen, and civilian leaders whom I had the honor to train, lead, and serve with, I bow to you. I have seen your resolve and your spirit. You are the nation's most precious treasure.

And to the Creator, who knows all things and who sparked a flame in my heart for service, I owe it all to you.

José A. LugoSantiago

INTRODUCTION

———

Longing for Authentic Leaders

On a Thursday morning, a few days before Christmas, I went to the local store to get a battery charger for my phone. The stores were crowded with people. Everyone was trying to get the good holiday deals, do the last-minute shopping before Christmas, and get back home as soon as they could.

I knew that when I started driving to the store. That's why I developed a shopping strategy. As any good tactician would do, my strategy was to picture in my mind exactly what I wanted, infiltrate the store like some kind of Special Forces agent, and then get out quickly, unseen!

I arrived at the store promptly as my well-carved plan dictated. But then my well-carved plan met reality. Between the parking lot and the store entrance, I met friends, colleagues, and even some people I had not seen in years. Finally, after almost an hour, I was able to move into the electronics department—so much for my strategy!

There they were. Hanging on the store rack, side by side, were the cell phone chargers. My phone's manufacturer built one of them; another company built the other, the alternate. I compared the prices, made a calculated decision—at least that's what I thought—and bought the alternate.

When I got home, I took the charger out of its packaging, plugged it in, and hooked my phone to it. An hour later, I checked. The phone's battery was dead. Not only did the phone charger not work, but when I took the charger off the wall, it came apart. I could not believe it! "I should have bought the original," I lamented.

Would buying the original have had a better fate? I think so! How could I have known? I could not have. I did have a feeling, though, that the original was going to be better. Why this obsession with buying or insisting on having the authentic one and not a copycat of it? Have you thought about that? I did—especially that day!

Authenticity brings a certain kind of peace of mind and confidence to us that the thing we're buying will deliver as expected. It's some sort of reputation we believe will be repeatable, and so we buy into it, sometimes without even thinking about it.

It's the same in leadership. We want authentic leaders, the real deal, the original. When we find authentic leaders, we believe in them and we follow them. When they make decisions, we seldom question them. When they demand a ton, we give a ton! In short, we subscribe to them without thinking too much about why we do so. We just know that they are the real deal, and therefore, deserve our support.

The truth is that there is a shortage of authentic leaders. Most workplaces today are filled with followers who long for authentic leaders. Tell me, who wants to work for a person who's rude, is full of self-interest, does not inspire trust, and is, in your opinion, not cut out to be a leader? The so-called leader I just described is the nightmare of any worker or workplace. Those so-called leaders drain dry the imagination and productivity of people and organizations. It's a terrible thing.

Watch out! You can be one of them. If you don't have the heart and mind to be an authentic leader, you most likely are one of those so-called leaders. And everyone in your workplace knows about it except you!

> You can only get oranges from the orange tree.
>
> ~Grandmother Elba

My grandmother was right, and her words apply in the context of leadership too. Great leaders produce great leadership in the workplace. That's why people and organizations thrive around great leaders. You need to be a great, authentic leader.

I wrote this book because I want you to be an authentic leader. I could have taken this book and made it full of strategic planning, project management, six sigma, or other how-to concepts. However, to tell you the truth, that's not what today's leaders need.

The biggest crisis of today is hollow, empty leaders. Many so-called leaders today know about strategic planning, for example, but can't compel the will of their followers. They must rely on positional power to get things done. Those so-called leaders lack the heart and mind of a leader, and therefore, lack authenticity. That's a crisis!

I want to help you and those you lead, really! If you're a senior leader, you may want to give this book a thorough look. After twenty-five years of experience leading, advising, studying, coaching, and growing leaders, I find that the people who need the biggest piece of advice are senior leaders. If you're a junior or aspiring leader, you're already on good footing—congratulations! Regardless of whether you're a senior or young leader, practicing the principles in this book will make you authentic—the leader we all long for.

Since authentic leadership consists of the heart and mind working in concert, I have divided this book into three parts. The first part deals with the heart. Specifically, it's about developing the courage leaders need to be decisive, to avoid just being another number in a crowd, to be resilient, to be open to others, and to be strong.

The second part of this book is about developing the mind of an authentic leader. The aim is to build toughness in character. Developing your mind means to harness the instinct to see beyond the obvious.

The last part meshes both heart and mind. This is the complete leader: one who can harmonize the passion of the heart with the instinct and intellect of the mind. Let's get started!

Lugo

I. ONE STRONG HEART

Building Courage

———

The heart is the source of a person's power. From it, all things flow: serenity and fury; love and hate; attraction and deflection; misery and happiness; energy and inability. Somehow, what we hold in our hearts flow into the physical world. Of course! The outward expression is a reflection of the internal makeup.

Courage, which resides in the heart, is the source of a leader's power. If we are to express courage and energize everything around us, we must cultivate courage in our hearts.

This section is comprised of eight small stories designed to help you understand what courage is so you can cultivate it. Read one story a day. Then let the ideas expressed in the story settle in your heart before moving on to the next. Onward!

Facing Goliath, Again![1]

You already have every characteristic necessary for success if you recognize, claim, develop and use them.

~Zig Ziglar

---

[1] Art printed with permission of its creator, Homero Ruiz Garcia, artist and illustrator. Copyright 2015.

I remember sitting as a young boy at a youth gathering. All of us, young boys and girls, were assembled in a circle so we could hear and talk to each other. Our youth leader began reading the story of David and Goliath.

As many of you know, David, a young boy, confronted Goliath on the battlefield.[2] Goliath was a scary, fully armored, war-experienced, giant fighter who promised to devour David and give his remains to the birds.

David had many reasons to be afraid and hide with the multitude of others who were also afraid of Goliath. Instead, David decided he was not going to tolerate that type of talk against his people and went out to the field to confront Goliath. With five rocks in his sack and a sling, he stepped out to the field. It took courage, one rock in the sling, precise aim, and motion to bring down Goliath.

Throughout the years, I've heard that story countless times. I am still captivated by the significance of this story in our modern times. Maybe you are too.

---

[2] 1 Samuel 17, *The Bible*, New International Version.

I've also seen Goliath in the "battlefield" many times. I've been afraid. Sometimes I've been able to conquer that fear and come through. Other times, I've not done so well. Many times, I've asked the skies about the reason why Goliath reappeared. I just wanted my path clear. I held malice toward none! Why didn't he go away?

As the years passed, I began to understand the significance of Goliath and its blessing. First, there is no way we would have known about David if it were not for his encounter with Goliath. Goliath was David's blessing for sure, his opportunity to show what courage could do. Thereafter, people clearly recognized who David was. It is the same for you and every leader who faces surmounting difficulties. Goliath is the blessing! Your encounter with him will highlight who you really are and what you're really made of.

The second point about Goliath and his significance as a blessing is showcased in David's actions. Now on the battlefield, he was ultimately responsible for defeating Goliath. There was no passing of the baton to another person. David had to quickly account for the assets at his disposal and his own personal capabilities. Then he had to combine them effectively to defeat Goliath, regardless of what the people were saying or how much more prepared his opponent appeared to be. David stepped out into the field, spoke to Goliath with confidence, and looked in his sack. He had five rocks and a sling. He employed his own talent and the few tools he had (actually just one rock), and defeated Goliath.

Here's the key question for you as the leader: What do you have that can help you defeat your Goliath? Look in your sack (your heart) to see what you can find. Find the courage to be bold and use what you're gifted with. If you find at least one rock, that's all you need.

Courage matters dearly. Courage is the power that makes you see the potential of your gifts and talents. If you have courage, then you'll unravel a world of opportunities. If you lack courage, you'll turn blind to the world of opportunities and certainly your own future. I know many people with great abilities and intelligence, but they lack courage. Since they lack courage, they also lack the power to change their lives. Consequently, they spend their time complaining about how they don't make progress.

I want you to look in your sack for a brief moment, or just feel for a moment what's in it. I bet you'll find at least one rock named passion. Affix it to your sling and have the courage to give it momentum. Here's an example of what happens when courage begins to give your passion some momentum.

Oprah is well known as a talk show host, actress, television producer, philanthropist, and more. Although admired for her success, she's also an inspiration to millions for her innate ability to harness her own passion, and that of others, battle the giants, and create massive success. Although she was already a renowned talk show host, she knew there was more. She brought her passion for reading and mentoring into her show, making her goal to have audiences find inspiration through reading a reality. Her show became a multi-million dollar publishing platform.[3] In 2011, she launched her own TV network.[4] And the rest, as it is said in popular circles, is history.

---

[3] Deahl, Rachel. "Bidding (an Early) Adieu to the Book Club Queen." *Publishers Weekly* 256, no. 48 (November 30, 2009): 4.
[4] Oprah Winfrey Biography: America's Beloved Best Friend, Academy of Achievement, last modified August 31, 2015, http://www.achievement.org/autodoc/page/win0bio-1

Many other examples exist, but I think you can catch my purpose. The main thing is that you don't get paralyzed by a scary situation and allow that situation to take away the opportunity to demonstrate how courage can overcome and unleash the passions that lead to unlimited success.

Just as David used all he had (five rocks and a sling) to defeat Goliath, you too can exercise courage to use your own gifts and defeat the Goliath in your life. Goliath will then be your blessing, a true account of what courage can overcome, and your step onto something incredible in your future. Harnessing courage is the first step to becoming the leader we want to follow.

The Giant Mirror

I n Disney's *Snow White*, the beautiful queen would stand in front of the magic mirror and ask, "Mirror, mirror on the wall, who's the fairest of them all?" And the mirror always replied, "My Queen, you are the fairest one of all." The response always pleased the queen because the mirror could not lie.

Although a fairy tale, we can learn much from the actions of the queen and the relationship between the mirror and our inner and outer world. The mirror, for example, is a very mysterious thing. It reflects outwardly the thoughts, feelings, perceptions, and sometimes the struggles, inside of us, whether we like it or not. It never lies.

Most of us have at least one or two mirrors in our homes. Many carry small mirrors in their purses and wallets. While traveling, I remember seeing a young woman using her cell phone as a mirror—we've really gone digital! Seems like the mirror has come to be an important part of who we are and the image of ourselves we want to see. To that end, the mirror brings a sense of affirmation. We seek to see an image of ourselves, and we seek affirmation.

> Cricket [the young boy] smiled and the pond smiled.
> Cricket stuck out his tongue and the pond did likewise.
> "That's the way the world works, too," Grandpa
> explained. "It will simply cast back the reflection you
> show it first."
>
> ~The Tiny Warrior[5]

---

[5] D. J. Eagle Bear Vanas, *The Tiny Warrior: A Path to Personal Discovery and Achievement* (Kansas City, MO: Andrews McMeel Publishing, 2003).

Most amazingly, when we don't carry the mirror with us, the world around us becomes a giant mirror just like in the experience of the young boy Cricket. Sometimes we like the reflection; sometimes we don't. But just like in the instance of Cricket, the world is not shy to reflect back to us the image we've put in it.

We reflect to the world the abundance of our hearts. An abundance of thankfulness or happiness, for example, makes you say thank you and sparks your smile. An abundance of courage, integrity, and humanity makes you care for what you believe is right and makes you care for others. That which you give, you will also get back. In other words, you will always give from the abundance of you.

People sometimes get discouraged when they see a person committing transgressions. Although unfortunate, I don't. Remember that the abundance of that person's heart has revealed his nature. And if that person ends up having success, don't envy that success because history has shown it will be short-lived. When the hour of judgment comes—and it will come—don't be happy for that person's fall either. As a leader, you must fill your heart with something else, so you can be the leader that shines the light other need to see.

Instead, cultivate yourself so you can have abundance. Fill your heart with joy every day by seeking to do what's right. Don't do what's right because a reward may come sooner or later. Do it because it is in your heart to do. That is all.

> The thing that we need in the world today is a group of men and women who will stand up for right and be opposed to wrong, wherever it is.
>
> ~Martin Luther King Jr. [6]

It's sometimes tough to find what's right and then do it, especially when you think that your actions may label you as an outcast. One has to cultivate strength in the heart so strength flows from oneself naturally, particularly when the strength is needed most.

Start cultivating strength by committing to the struggle you will face because of your decision to be an authentic, real leader not ordinary nor someone who

---

[6] Martin Luther King Jr. and Carson Clayborne, "Boston University," *The Autobiography of Martin Luther King, Jr* (New York: Grand Central Publishing, 1998), 32–33.

will conform to mediocrity. This means you will have to exercise excellence as a value in your personal behavior by practicing diligence in self-mastery, and by practicing total professionalism in your craft until the practice becomes habit.

Self-mastery is true greatness. Pursue it! It's about sharpening yourself over your life's journey through the cultivation of moral values. The practice of values under pressure and in difficult situations will make you stronger. Visualizing how you would practice your values in the toughest situations before you encounter them will make you stronger. In short, self-mastery will produce an abundance of strength and courage.

Professionalism is the outward expression of self-mastery. As a leader, most people will know you for who you are while you're in the position of leadership. Your outward expression of how you conduct your business should be the reflection of self-mastery. This means that you have the strength to handle conflict without becoming irate (a display of self-control that speaks about respect for self and others). You're not quick at losing your temper, and you're a master at balancing patience with voracious action.

Cultivate yourself so you can cast the right image of what you want to see in the world. The moment will soon come when your reflection will become the force that will encourage others and change everything. That's when you'll be known as an authentic leader—the one we long to follow!

Courage and Fear

So a certain degree of fear is necessary to the formation of true courage. All that is meant here is, that no habit of courage or self-mastery can be said to be matured, until pain altogether vanishes.

~Aristotle, *The Ethics of Aristotle*

Why didn't John correct his boss, who was acting unprofessionally? He expected me to do it. When the young man saw the senior leader violating simple rules of professional conduct, the young man hesitated to correct her. But the young man came to tell me. When the senior leader decided to depart from a clear directive, only two witnesses decided to confront her. Why couldn't someone take the leadership role and make these course corrections?

Is the cause a lack of courage? Is it fear of the potential social or career consequences the issue? Most people would not say anything. Actually, researchers estimate that 85% of executives are afraid to raise concerns in the workplace[7] and seven out of ten would not say anything even when the leader was about to make a wrong decision.[8] Aristotle's quote says something about courage we already know, right? Courage without fear is not courage. And bravery that sees no struggle is not courage either. Then he says that true courage is only born after we've passed through the stages of pain. There's no crown of bravery unless one has endured the pain of crawling the distance of time

---

[7] TED Global: Ideas worth spreading (Producer). (2012, June). *Margaret Heffernan: Dare to disagree.* Retrieved from http://www.ted.com/talks/margaret_heffernan_dare_to_disagree?language=en

[8] Bennis, W. (1999). The end of leadership: Exemplary leadership is impossible without full inclusion, initiatives, and cooperation of followers. *Organizational Dynamics*, 28(1), 78-79.

and space for what is right. Doing that, in most cases, involves journeying through disappointment, loneliness, and sometimes hopelessness.

For the leader who struggles, worried, feeling a certain degree of fear, let me highlight that the struggle is necessary to form strength in the heart: authenticity. One has to endure to earn the crown of courage and not the other way around (wear the crown to endure). One has to last through the fear and pain that sometimes occur when one decides to act based on deep-rooted beliefs. When one does, courage is born within us. This is the way of natural things.

Here are two examples. The earth must be disrupted before the plant is born. The young plant, which seeks the earth's sunlight to grow and blossom, has to pierce through the heavy earth covering it. The way a mother brings life into this world is another telling example. The mother brings a child into this world understanding that she will endure great pain, but her courage will be crowned with life, joy, and happiness. The pain is necessary; enduring it brings new life.

All of this sounds logical and even "touchy-feely" for some. Still, many in leadership positions shy away from demonstrating the moral courage we all want to see in leadership today. I guess this is not as touchy-feely as some think. Why the fear? It's the fear of being excluded from the "in-group," becoming unpopular that stops many "leaders" from discovering and allowing courage to be born in them. If that will make you hesitate, the great Emperor and Philosopher Marcus Aurelius, who ruled Rome during the years 161 to 180 AD, left us with some meaningful words of advice: "It can ruin your life only if it ruins your character. Otherwise it cannot harm you—inside or outside."[9]

All of us, as leaders, regardless of profession or position, face difficulty. It's necessary. The difficulties test our mettle, so you, as the leader, should not fear, but face difficulties with a big dose of optimism. Therein lies the opportunity for beauty and success. Don't let fear consume you. Overcome your fear; meet fear with action and courage. Only then will the courageous leader we long to follow be born.

---

[9] Marcus Aurelius and Gregory Hays, "Book 4," *Marcus Aurelius Meditations* (New York: Modern Library, 2002), 39.

How Do I Know What's Right?

Are we disposed to be of the number of those who, having eyes, see not, and, having ears, hear not...?

~Patrick Henry, March 23, 1775

Seems to me that in discussions of displaying courage, almost every time, an internal monologue emerges that prompts a very important question: How do I know what's right? The answer is not always clear. If you find yourself, as a leader, asking this question, you're certainly not alone.

This is the recurring question humanity has struggled to find the answer to since the beginning of time. The question appeared to great leaders at crucial intersections throughout history, and great leaders had to face life-or-death struggles to find the answer.

Founding father and governor of Virginia, Patrick Henry, pondered this question in 1775, when our forming nation was undecided as to whether to mobilize for a war for independence. How did he respond to the dilemma: Should we fight or not? (How do I know what's right?)

As one reads his "Give Me Liberty or Give Me Death" speech, key thoughts help highlight the thought process to find the answer to that burning question (what's right?).

> I consider [the question] as nothing less than a question of freedom or slavery.

Although his words in the preceding quote point to the actual debate of the colonies, to make a decision about breaking free or accept being subjugated to unjust laws, I believe the words resonate in our current leadership journey. When we are morally confronted with deciding what's right and what's not, the course forward may point to two outcomes: break free or stay subject to whatever your situation is.

I believe this is the fork in the road, and one has to decide where to go. Analyze then how given courses of action either set you free or preserve an unfavorable situation, limiting progress toward the future you (or your team) have the potential to own.

[I]t is natural to man to indulge in the illusions of hope. We are apt to shut our eyes against a painful truth, and listen to the song of that siren till she transforms us into beasts.

Another point in getting to the answer of what's right is conviction. Sometimes we decide not to move forward for fear the consequences may be too great. Still, we hear our inner giant voice, which knows best, telling us, "Go! Act on your sense of conviction; that's the path."

If you've sensed that something inside of you is insistently talking to you, that's probably the voice of conviction. Take the advice. Listen to the voice of conviction, and then talk with those good friends who can give you counsel.

Remember that whatever course of action you take, you will not be able to escape the consequences. You might as well take action that aligns with the path that leads to personal freedom and answers your senses of conviction. This exact point is termed in popular language as crossing the Rubicon.

In ancient times, Julius Cesar became known as a victorious leader and grew even more popular as the Roman governor of the Gaul province. He became so popular that the Roman senate in Italy felt threatened by him. The senate issued a message: resign and disband your army, or be killed.

Julius decided to go to Rome and settle the dispute. Crossing the Rubicon, the small river that divided the province of Gaul and Italy, was the decision point. He pondered the question thoroughly. He knew that once he crossed, there was no return. He crossed the river with his army and sparked a civil war, which he won. His actions also sparked a series of events that ended his life years after he was emperor but transformed the world until this day.

Are you at that point where you could cross the Rubicon? Listen to your sense of conviction. Gather the courage to cross the Rubicon. You're probably stronger than you think.

> They tell us, sir, that we are weak; unable to cope with so formidable an adversary. But when should we be stronger?

Similarly, Patrick Henry found it was time for our nation to cross the Rubicon. Many doubted that the nation had the strength. Little did the doubters know that they were not outnumbered. They were not outnumbered because courage that overcomes fear is more powerful than the prison of hope that sees no action. The rest, as you know, is history.

Finding what's right was a debate between slavery and liberty for Patrick Henry.[10] It could be the same for you—a decision of whether to accept staying subjugated or promoting a course of action that gives you freedom and genuine power.

---

[10] Henry, James, *The Ambassadors* (1909; Project Gutenberg, 1996), bk. 6, Chap. 1, ftp://ibiblio.org/pub/docs/books/gutenberg/etext96/ambas10.txt

Finding what's right means getting to the Rubicon and then mustering the courage to cross it. It could be the same for you—realize that in your heart you may already feel you've reached a critical juncture; to postpone doing what's right is not going to make it better. Seek advice when you need to, but then cross the Rubicon. If you can do that, then you'll become a courageous leader, followed by legions who will trust you and fight for you.

"Because I Was Strong, I Became Stronger."

We're creating an environment where everything is too rosy because everyone is afraid to paint the true picture. You just wonder where it will break, when it will fall apart.

~Wong and Gerras[11]

---

[11] L. Wong and S. Gerras, *Lying to Ourselves: Dishonesty in the Army Profession*, Strategic Studies Institute (Carlisle, PA: US Army War College Press, 2015), 28.

How do you deal with making course corrections or giving feedback when things are going wrong? The person who can do this is the one who has a heart for leadership. Many people plainly avoid getting involved and try to ignore the unpleasant situation. The problem is that not making a correction or giving appropriate feedback will not make a bad situation go away.

In over two decades of observing good and bad leadership, I have never seen a bad situation turn into a good one by leaving it alone. Usually, the situation gets worse. I've watched how little things slowly begin to creep up and eat away at the good culture of organizations, to the point where people no longer enjoy coming to work, even suffering illnesses just thinking about coming to work. How is it that the power of a multitude of good people can't fix the problem one or two bad people created? Why didn't someone take the role of leader to change the situation?

The nature of human beings is to avoid pain and seek pleasure. If something is going to be painful, we avoid it, sometimes not thinking that our involvement, painful as it could be for a moment, could turn pain into lasting joy. It's natural; we want to avoid unpleasant moments. I know I've been guilty of that at times too. Let me give you a short personal example.

In 2015 I relocated from the Washington, DC, area to San Antonio, Texas. While in the process, my family and I vacated our old house and stayed in a hotel. On the second day in the hotel, my wife and I complained to each other about the noise the upstairs neighbors were making: late-night disturbances and a squeaky floor that sometimes woke us up in the middle of our sleep.

I mentioned it to the clerk, but since we had one more night left, my wife and I decided to endure the situation. The checkout day came quickly. During the checkout and after I paid for the hotel, the receptionist handed me the receipt, and with a smile asked, "How was your stay with us?"

Many thoughts came to mind. How should I answer? Will I fix anything by telling her? Didn't I already tell her about the problem? Well, with a polite smile I answered, "All good, ma'am. Thank you," and walked to my car.

As I began driving, I thought about why I had done that. I rationalized the excuses, but deeply I knew I should have spoken to the clerk, once again, about the problem. Did I make it better? No. Will it be better for the next person? No. What did I have to lose? Nothing. Maybe I should have told her, politely, that she needed to stay in that room a few nights to understand the problem.

In other personal examples where I have taken the leader's role, I remember tactfully correcting out-of-character behavior of senior executives and also correcting lack of adherence to written standards by troops high and low in the chain of command (from simple uniform violations to the use of profanity in public). Despite thoughtful and tactful application of several methods, the result was not always an appreciation for what standards could do for an organization. But every time, bystanders came to thank me for getting involved. Of course, none of them carried the scars of the personal consequences that I sometimes had to bear as the result of those confrontations and my intentions to set a good example for others to follow.

The situation I just described almost always raises the following questions: Why didn't the bystander become the leader? Or why didn't the leader become the courageous leader?

> Self-deception causes the moral implications of a decision to fade, allowing individuals to behave incomprehensibly and, at the same time, not realize that they are doing so.
>
> ~Professor Ann Tenbrunsel[12]

Many times, I've attributed the creeping of ethical fading as the answer to those questions. The leader, witnessing the behavior, becomes surprised by the inappropriate behavior. Quickly, as he examines himself, he finds emptiness (a lack of courage) within himself and begins his own process of self-deception. The leader begins to tell himself why what he saw was not so bad. Then he begins to rationalize why he needed to leave it alone and how not getting involved was the best course of action.

---

[12] A. Tenbrunsel and D. Messick, "Ethical Fading: The Role of Self-Deception in Unethical Behavior," *Social Justice Journal* 17, no. 2 (2004): 224.

Ethical fading is one good explanation; another explanation deals with the quandary a leader faces when at the fork in the road. In my previous book, *On the Leadership Journey: 30 Conversations about Leading Yourself and Others,*[13] I wrote a story titled "Inner Civil War, Moment of Truth, and Fork in the Road." In it, I explained, through an example, how each of us goes through three emotional stages in deciding what to do, especially in finding the courage to confront inappropriate behavior.

Let me recap the story. The inner civil war is your internal personal struggle (just like the one I described previously). The moment of truth is the discovery of who you are and want to be. And the fork in the road is the decision point—aware of possible personal consequences, you decide to either go the easy way or take the rocky way in the fork.

In matters of consequence, I believe the decision point at the fork is what really makes the difference between authentic leaders and ordinary people. Without realizing it, the fork in the road is more about making a

---

[13] J. LugoSantiago, *On the Leadership Journey: 30 Conversations about Leading Yourself and Others* (Wajbook Press, 2014), 19–23.

choice to become morally and ethically stronger or become just another number in the crowd (a passive observer and victim of whatever someone else has planned for your life).

Making tough decisions at the fork matters. In early May 2015 I delivered a talk on the topic of empowerment to a large crowd in DC. After the talk, some people stayed behind to chat with me about their experiences. One of them told me her personal story; I was moved. She remembered being at the fork in the road many times. Each time, she made the conscious, tough decision to become the leader and take the rocky way to the mountain road. With every tough decision, her courage became stronger. Her position as a leader became influential, and she became the de facto trusted advisor in the workplace and the community. Because she was strong (strong to display courage), she became stronger.

Becoming stronger is a matter of choice. When you find yourself at the fork, find courage and make the right choice to display it. In the end, you'll overcome your fears, become stronger, and transform into the leader we all want to follow.

José A. LugoSantiago

Walking on the Street

Some people live consumed with their own world, and can't see how their actions endanger themselves and others. This is especially widespread in leaders who take for granted how their decisions or indecisions affect their ability to lead and endanger their team's performance. Do you know of a few examples? Let me take a few lines to explain.

On an early, cold winter morning, I drove to work. As I got close to my office building, I left the main road and entered the parking lot. The speed limit in the parking lot was 10 mph. That seemed like a safe speed, especially considering that there may be ice on the pavement and one is sure to encounter pedestrians. And I can always count on encountering pedestrians in the parking lot, but in the middle of the street?

On that day, I encountered a person walking in the middle of the street. He appeared to move to the left, and then quickly changed directions and moved to the right. He did that a few times, and meanwhile, I was driving slowly behind him to allow him time to decide which way to go. I'm thinking, "Is he aware of the dangers?" I stopped my car.

I wondered if the person heard my car's engine. No, he didn't. Once the person changed directions again and decided to walk on the left side, I was able to slowly pass the person and park my vehicle. I got out of the car and walked toward the person. I needed to talk with the person about the dangers of his indecision.

As I was walking toward the person, I thought about Mr. Miyagi. In the famous 1984 movie *The Karate Kid*, Mr. Miyagi taught young Daniel-san several life lessons on his journey to learn karate. One of them is about walking on the street. And it goes something like this:

Mr. Miyagi: Now, ready?

Daniel-san: Yeah, I guess so.

Mr. Miyagi (sighs): Daniel-san, must talk.

They look at each other and both kneel.

Mr. Miyagi: Walk on road, hmm? Walk left side, safe. Walk right side, safe. Walk middle, sooner or later (*makes squish gesture*) get squish just like grape. Here, karate, same thing. Either you karate do yes or karate do no. You karate do "guess so," (*makes squish gesture*) just like grape. Understand?

When I think about that dialogue, I think about leadership and courage. It's a powerful message for leaders. The message is this: have the courage to make decisions; your life's success, your team's success, and your organization's safety depend on it! Flip-flopping as a leader exasperates followers. No one likes to be led by a leader who cannot make up his or her mind. Be courageous; take a stand please: walk on the right or walk on the left!

The consequence of indecisions can be substantial personally and organizationally. For example, not making up your mind as to whether to take on an important life project diminishes your chances to achieve personal goals; you'll just wander in the abyss of time confused and without the ability to focus your energy to overcome obstacles. And if there will be people involved, they will be consumed by desperation, waiting for you to make a decision. But since those people will lose confidence in you, they will put their energies and faith in someone (and something) else. In other words, as a leader, you've lost your followers—you're no longer the leader.

Moreover, if you have the bad habit of constantly walking in the middle of the street, not exercising the courage to take the left or the right side on make-or-break issues, sooner or later you will become irrelevant in your organization. In life, you have to stand for something. What do you stand for? Exercise that faculty (strong will and courage) and stand for something. Who knows? You may change the course of history. We all know someone who did!

President Abraham Lincoln knew a thing or two about taking a stand. The US Civil War would have had a very different outcome if he had decided to walk in the middle of the street or to flip-flop on issues when he was faced with violent opposition. It's only fitting to heed his words of wisdom.

> Some single mind must be master, else there will be no agreement in anything.[14]

When he said those words, he was referring to his firm position about General Steele commanding troops on the field and the president's resolute stance about not postponing elections for the State of Arkansas in 1864. With those words, he was delineating direction on two issues. One of them was about governance as a political leader and the other was about governance as the commander in chief of the military. The president's situation was complex. He was facing tremendous

---

[14] *The Collected Works of Abraham Lincoln*, ed. Roy P. Basler (New Brunswick, NJ: Rutgers University Press, 1953).

pressure from both the political and military fronts. It would have been very easy for him to walk in the middle of the street and change direction as things heated up. Imagine if that would have been the case: he would have lost politically and militarily.

You may not be facing make-or-break issues similar to those of President Lincoln, but in many respects, the core of the battles we face are all the same. Taking a stand as a leader ensures unity of purpose and gets work accomplished expediently. Taking a stand also ensures you build a culture of doing the right thing no matter how unpopular those decisions can sometimes be. Taking a stand whether to walk on the right side or the left side also builds confidence in your leadership and inspires your people to act with confidence—trust!

In an era where a few people have decided to walk in the middle of the street, you have to be the one to inspire decision-making. Be courageous and take a stand. If you can muster the courage to decide which side of the street to walk on when confronted with tough challenges, you will become the leader we want to follow.

Courage to See What Others Can't

Whatever course of action you decide upon, there is always someone to tell you, you are wrong.

There are always difficulties which tempt you to believe that you are wrong.

~Ralph Waldo Emerson

I f you've been a leader, I'm sure the previous quote is all too familiar to your journey. I don't know of any great leader who, in pursuit of truth or positive change, has not been told he or she was wrong. And in his or her journey, I don't know of any great leader who has not doubted the path he or she has taken.

Sometimes we find ourselves in circumstances where we grapple with the truth. We know what the truth is. In those moments, we ask ourselves the deep questions just to see if our moral compass still points in the same direction. Nevertheless, we continue to look for clues in our environment to validate what we already know is right.

It's even tougher when we look in our environment for clues, and all we see are mixed signals. In our environment, when we see people (and even leaders who are supposed to set the example) whose words and actions don't match, when we see that masked self-interest begins to take the center stage, what do we do?

A few months ago, a struggling leader confided in me, saying, "I don't know what to do. Sometimes I ask myself, 'Am I the only one who cares around here?' I can't be the only one seeing we're heading in the wrong direction." I pondered his concern and remembered seeing myself in his situation, asking myself the same question.

I remember asking my mentors for the best way to approach those difficult moments. Maybe I was trying to avoid the inevitable: conflict! I remember many of those times praying for guidance for the best way to manage difficult situations. Maybe I was trying not to rock the boat too much. I remember reading books about how to win friends and influence people, to find a way to best convince others about what my convictions were telling me. Maybe I was trying to avoid being outcasted by a majority who, after thinking deeply, were cemented in the comfort of their old ways and lacked the character to change.

Leadership requires courage. The true leader is born in the difficult moments and shaped by them. You've heard the saying, "No pressure, no diamonds." It's true! If you don't confront the difficult, you'll never realize the strength within you. Your strength will never develop, and you will not have the heart to be a leader.

And one other thing—the world will miss out on your contribution because fortune has been waiting for people who have the courage to drive change!

When you hear the multitude of voices telling you how wrong you are, and how you don't have this or that, think about the following examples:

Television won't be able to hold on to any market it captures after the first six months. People will soon get tired at staring at a plywood box every day.

~Daryl Zanuck, Twentieth Century Fox, 1946

There is no reason for any individual to have a computer in their home.

~Kenneth Olson, Digital Equipment Corporation, 1977

Everyone's always asking me when Apple will come out with a cell phone. My answer is, "Probably never."

~David Pogue, *The New York Times*, 2006

Do you know what I learned from the quotes above? Courage is necessary to see what others can't. A person with courage is a leader with vision. And when the courageous step outside of groupthink and bet on his or her ideas, there will be no shortage of people to tell the courageous they are wrong.

Over time, those people who opposed you and told you how this or that could not be done change. But the prerequisites for that change are knowing what's right and then having the courage to do it consistently. I once heard someone tell me the truth goes through three stages. First, it is violently opposed. Secondly, it is studied, doubted, and debated (gaining, after thought, proponents and opponents). And finally, it is accepted. History is full of examples.

What does this discussion mean to you now as a leader? Simple. Search for what's right, and when you have found the direction in your heart, go do it with a courageous heart (I'll explain how in Part III of this book.) You'll be opposed, but don't wobble in the valley of despair or surrender your purpose. As you start walking on your personal leadership journey, somewhere along the way, you'll begin to feel inspired by the footprints you'll see. Yes, other great leaders have also walked that same road; those are their footprints, and they became the leaders we all wanted to follow.

José A. LugoSantiago

The Eye of the Storm

W hen the elements of nature produce the imbalance that creates thunder, rain, and devastating winds, deeply inside emerges the power (peace, quietness, and blue skies) that takes control and guides the storm. Just like in the eye of a hurricane, so it is in the leader's heart. In the inner peace and quietness of the heart, the leader begins to harness the power that takes control of the storm that surrounds him. That's what I've learned in nature and continue to see in leadership. Let me explain this parallel through personal experience and then relate this natural phenomenon to the innate lesson in building a real, authentic leader.

Growing up in an island, my family and I survived several hurricanes, some recorded as most devastating in the modern history of the Caribbean. When I think about those moments, I remember seeing myself as a curious, young boy trying to figure out why nature was so angry.

As a family, we prepared. We stored water and food, nailed wood and aluminum panels to protect the windows, chained heavy objects, and kept pace with the news to track the storm's path. When the inevitable became evident, the "mad giant" would enter the island with all his might turning off all power—total blackout. We listened intensely to the news through a battery-operated radio. At times, the radio signal would disappear; the sounds of the pounding wind, the radiance of lightning, and the shaking from the unbearable explosion of thunder were the only noises left. During the moments of the storm, when the winds were blowing hard and one could hear the collisions of flying objects, we would worry about our loved ones: Will they make it?

The wind would blow hard for hours wanting to tip over the house. When the wind could not do it, the rain would come hard trying to succeed at the work the wind couldn't finish. And when neither of them were successful (or even when the partnership between wind and rain could not do the job), the thunder would announce loudly the mad giant's rage, angry because he could not complete the devastation. Then everything would cease. The rain and the clouds would disappear. The winds would take a break, and the skies would turn clear, beautiful, and blue.

Escaping my mother's eyes one of those times when everything had ceased, I ventured outside to feel and hear nature. Being outside felt like being inside a soundproof room: deep, quiet, weird on the ears...unreal. However, the most overwhelming feeling I had was one of peace. As my mother rushed me inside the house (and sternly lectured me) after being caught sneaking out, I asked her if the storm was over. I wondered why it was so peaceful and so great out in the open. She said, "No, it's not over, honey; that's just how it feels when you're in the eye of the storm."

Hurricanes are a fascinating phenomenon. They are the most violent storms on Earth, and although they form through the movement of warm and moist air, hurricanes do not take on their full, devastating power until the formation of an eye. Scientific research has observed that the formation of the eye leads to the hurricane's ability to orchestrate the motion of the winds, low and high-pressure zones, heavy rain, and cloud formations, maintaining and intensifying the structure of the storm.[15] The eye becomes the mastermind of the storm once it is formed. The eye, the most peaceful and clear place in the storm, is crucial to the hurricane's power. The same can be said about the leader.

As the eye is the center of the hurricane, so is the heart the center of the leader. The leader must develop the heart, so it can produce centralization of the leader's powers. When you can achieve centralization, outside

---

[15] Vigh, Johnathan L., John A. Knaff, and Wayne H. Schubert, "A climatology of hurricane eye formation," *Monthly Weather Review – American Meteorology Society*, no. 140, (May 2012).

events or people cannot control your mood, your conditions, or your future. You become the force that orchestrates the destiny of the things around you. This centralization unifies and harmonizes your inner self and the other dimensions of your life—the physical, mental, spiritual, and social. Here are some things you should do to achieve centralization.

- Find silence and solitude. In the morning or before going to bed at night, go to a place where you can be alone. Find a comfortable position, close your eyes, and stay silent. In the beginning, you may feel overwhelmed with thoughts. Don't solve anything. Just stay silent and relaxed.

- Be grateful. This is the act of feeling and realizing your gifts. This is also the act of breaking free from anger, forgiving, and moving on. Do it.

- Visualize the leader in your heart. Think about and feel the kind of servant leader that you wish to be. See others as part of your team, even if they don't see themselves as part of yours. See yourself helping people overcome their insecurities. *Feel* yourself achieving these things.

- Discipline your mouth. The wise King Solomon counseled, "Guard your heart [...] and keep corrupt talk far from your lips."[16] Gandhi also exhorted, "Keep your words positive, because your words become your behavior." In the end, these things control your behavior, habits, values, and destiny.

- Get to work and put forth a sincere effort. Really, forget who takes the credit in your daily endeavors. Your effort should focus on works that become pieces of art. As you lead work activities, you don't need to remind anyone about how bad the day is, just turn it around and be happy the day is yours to have. You will attract what your words speak and what you give.

This is how you create the conditions for the emergence of a new kind of leader—the genuine, authentic leader we all long to follow. Achieve centrality by cultivating your heart. Become like the hurricane, able to control the storm through the inner peace and quietness of the heart.

---

[16] Proverbs 4:23-24, *The Bible*, New International Version.

II. ONE CLEVER MIND

Building Character

———

The first part of this book was about the heart of the leader: developing courage to produce energy and abundant power for action. However, a good heart without a good mind is like launching NASA's space shuttle into space without its navigational systems.

Therefore, in this second part, the stories are aimed at developing the mind of the leader because the mind is the creator. It charts the course for things to exist. It shapes how we see things, how we feel, and who we will be. James Allen, in his book, *As a Man Thinketh,* puts it this way: "A man cannot directly choose his circumstances, but he can choose his thoughts, and so indirectly, yet surely, shape his circumstances."[17]

---

[17] J. Allen, "Effect of Thought on Circumstances," *As a Man Thinketh* (Quezon City: New Century Books, 2010), 8.

If you can develop your mind, then you can control and shape your destiny. Then you can become the leader we want to follow. Let's begin.

The Wolf and the Lion: Achieving Awareness

Roaming by the mountainside at sundown, a Wolf saw his own shadow become greatly extended and magnified. He said to himself, "Why should I, being of such an immense size and extending nearly an acre in length, be afraid of the Lion?

Ought I not to be acknowledged as King of all the collected beasts?"

While he was indulging in these thoughts, a Lion fell upon him and killed him. He exclaimed with a too late repentance, "Worthless me! This overestimation of myself is the cause of my destruction."

~Aesop's The Wolf and the Lion[18]

Have you ever met a person whose demeanor and inner voice said, "We have not met before, but you should know how big and important I am"? Every time I've met that person, I've quickly discovered that person lacked not only humility but also self-awareness, a critical part of a leader's ability to think and influence. This gap in humility and self-awareness translates into the person's self-destruction.

Think for a second about the last statement I made. Have you ever heard or been in a situation where you met someone, let's say at a party, and bragged about yourself, only to find out the person you were talking to was a *really* important person? How about that for a

---

[18] *Aesop's Fables*, George Fyler Townsend, trans., Kindle, public domain, 68.

very first good impression? That's what I call self-destruction.

On the other hand, I've also met some of the most full-of-life, full-of-greatness people. If you would meet one of them on the street, you would not even notice. They're unassuming. But once you pay close attention or spend time with them, you discover they're happy, motivating, wise, and caring. When they meet you, they seem to have known you an entire lifetime. They're so happy to connect with you. They possess awareness: awareness of self (own gifts) and awareness of others (people's gifts and potential).

One thing I've learned is that the educated and wise would never meet another and boast of himself, convinced that he or she is of more worth than the other is. That doesn't happen. I've also learned that people of substance and worth would meet another human being and would feel humbled to have just found another friend. That's what happens to leaders who cultivate awareness.

Awareness is a different point of view. This trait in the leader sets the course for the discovery of talent in people. Each of us has innate talents and gifts. Some of us have powers we have not even discovered. For us to flourish, we need to make the right connection, meet the person with the right set of keys to unlock and open the doors of our own self-discovery.

The same is true for those followers the leader is charged with leading. They long for a leader who can discover them, who can see those innate gifts in them. Unfortunately, most times, the follower meets leaders who are consumed with themselves and can't see past their own supposed greatness. The follower's talents are left undiscovered, and that potentially amazing contribution is lost.

Who do you want to be? I am sure you don't want to be known as the self-consumed leader. It's more rewarding to be known as a leader who was sent to another human being for the sole purpose of unlocking the doors of that person's self-discovery.

Cultivate awareness in your leadership. Cultivating awareness is about an attitude that states, I am aware of my talents, but I live to discover and unleash the potential in others. Having awareness is about being wholly aware of your capacities and the reasons you were given special privileges as a leader. Those capacities, those gifts given to you, are yours for a reason.

It's not for you to boast about what has been given to you, fully unaware of the potential of those around you. Seek the best way possible to employ and share what has been given to you, so you can discover and unleash the potential of those you lead. You may hold the key to someone else's self-discovery. Go out and unlock his or her potential. If you do, you will be a leader.

José A. LugoSantiago

I Live for the Applause

The person who seeks all their applause from outside has their happiness in another's keeping.

~Dale Carnegie

wo leaders enter the arena of leadership. The first leader, upon getting direction, goes out and works intensely to meet the demands of the work given. Along the way, this leader encounters the opportunity to focus his effort: choose to appease the opposition or devote the energy to doing his duty, true to convictions, and faithful about successful outcomes. In the end, his highest praise comes from knowing the work done was through a team and done with utmost quality and precision. The second leader, upon getting direction, works intensely, ensuring the team stays committed to the task. The leader labors diligently but is preoccupied with how the outcome will open the door for other, more attractive opportunities. Both leaders accomplish the task with success.

When all is said and done, we all can easily identify who is the first and who is the second leader. The telling difference is their vocabulary. Leaders of the first kind tend to substitute "I" for "we." Leaders of the second kind tend to substitute "we" for "I." The spotlight must be totally on them rather than on the team. This is so common that even pop culture song lyrics remind us of the discord.

If you enjoy (or have heard) popular music, you've probably heard of Lady Gaga. Ok, I know what you're thinking! "How did she get into this leadership conversation?" All I can say is that one night I was listening to the lyrics of a particular song, and the thought came to mind. How did I connect Lady Gaga and leadership? Let me get to the point and tell you.

Lady Gaga, in the song, kept repeating, "I live for the applause, applause, applause." Well, it's somewhat catchy. I'm sure if you've heard the song, it is probably playing in your head right now, and you can't stop it. Her words reminded me of the type of leader who lives for the applause, the one who tends to substitute the "we" for the "I." How dangerous this is!

> Nearly all men can stand adversity, but if you want to test a man's character, give him power.
>
> ~Abraham Lincoln

Leaders who constantly enter ventures thinking, "What's in it for me?" are not real leaders. These people seek applause, glory, and popularity rather than seeking the transformation of their people and their organizations.

What's the problem? Leaders of this kind will avoid the tough decisions because those decisions may widen the gap between where they are and where they want to be (their self-interest). Additionally, leaders of this kind will not be open to constructive feedback. In turn, they surround themselves with those followers who can only praise and adore the leaders' presence. Remember, they are applause-leaders.

The actions just described create a terrible leadership environment, a self-deception box. First, courageous followers will be cast away. (Let me note that courageous followers are desperately needed in organizations. Without them, applause-leaders can't see the blind spots of their thinking and the unintended consequences of their decisions. Who else will tell applause-leaders to watch out?)

Secondly, applause-leaders split organizations and promote distrust. Two teams exist in organizations led by applause-leaders: the in-circle and everyone else. When the going gets tough, applause-leaders will seek the advice of the in-circle, those followers who provoke the applause (uncourageous followers), regardless if the actions of the applause-leaders are right or wrong. Because of this unilateral view on issues, the applause-leader and the members of the organization begin to live in two different realities. The view of the leader is that those who tell the truth are wrong, and the view of the members of the organization is that the leader is detached. The landscape becomes a battlefield where both factions fight for territory and their own safety. Ultimately, many good, creative, and hard-working people leave the organization.

My point here is not to belittle the applause-leader but to make you aware. Specifically, why did I get into this applause-leader discussion? Because I care about you! You may be a good leader, but if you don't watch yourself, you will be caught in this trap. The longer you remain a leader, and the higher you go up the leadership ladder, the greater the danger that you could become enamored with the applause, and in turn, become the applause-leader.

Trust me. I've been witness to this unfortunate metamorphosis where the leader begins to think he or she is funny, sexy, and even more intelligent than the combined brainpower of his or her team. It's a terrible thing! Don't let it be you.

> And there is deep down within all of us an instinct. It's a kind of major instinct—a desire to be out front, a desire to lead the parade, a desire to be first.
>
> ~Martin Luther King Jr.

That drum major instinct, as Dr. Martin Luther King calls it, that need for the applause and the spotlight, will call on you. It's okay. But that major drum instinct needs to be harnessed and aligned with a much higher purpose in your life. That purpose, as a leader, is to serve others: your family, your community, your institution. If you can understand this and act accordingly, then you will be a leader.

"Destroy the Ships!"

Hernán Cortés sailed from Cuba, landing in the Yucatán Peninsula with a fleet of eleven ships and some six hundred men. The year was 1519. Upon disembarking, the men joining Cortés quickly came to the realization that they were in a mysterious new land. Although the thought of gold, land, and glory was a motivator to embrace the exploration of this new land, these six hundred men were unsure of what awaited them. This mysterious land, they learned, was ruled by a powerful, warrior-like emperor. Success in this conquest meant complete devotion and focus, and Cortés knew this foremost.

The journey was going to be tough on that conquest. There were going to be times when these men were going to be hungry and tired, with an even greater desire to return home. Cortés already had to use severe measures to disband a plot in his camp.

Depressed with the circumstances, he assembled his most trusted leaders and unveiled his plan: "The ships must be destroyed." He understood this was the only way he could force his men to push forward with the exploration and further the conquest. And so, in secrecy, he went with his trusted leaders and dismantled the boats, all but one.

The news spread quickly through the camp. The men demanded an explanation for the harsh actions taken to destroy the only means to return to the world they knew. Cortés answered,

And what use would the ships have been to us? If we succeed, we shall not need them. If we fail, we shall be too far in the interior to reach the coast. Have confidence in yourselves, you have set your hands to the work; to look back is ruin![19]

Finding no way to move but forward, Cortés and his men moved inland, reached the capital of the Aztec empire, and in 1521, conquered the Aztecs.[20]

I can think of two other historic examples where burning the ships led to amazing conquests: Alexander the Great (334 BC), facing the Persians; and Tariq bin Ziyad (710 AD), facing the Visigoths in Spain. In both cases, these commanders were outnumbered at least six to one.

It seems that, in the history of humankind, whenever we find ourselves without alternatives, we find a way to overcome our challenges with overwhelming determination. Amazingly, and sometimes to our

---

[19] Margaret D. Coxhead, "Cortes Burns His Boats," *Romance of History: Mexico*, (London: TC and EC Jack, 1909), 96–97.
[20] Winston A. Reynolds, "The Burning Ships of Hernán Cortés," *Hispania* (American Association of Teachers of Spanish and Portuguese), 3rd ed., vol. 42 (1959): 317.

disbelief, we achieve these magnificent victories against all odds.

> Let us not be content to wait and see what will happen, but give us the determination to make the right things happen.
>
> ~Horace Mann

We can draw several important lessons from the previous story. First, if something honorable and magnificent must be achieved, give yourself and your team no other option but to achieve it. All of us know how easy it is to continue to do the same thing day after day. We know how easy it is to stay within the confines of the usual. The problem with the usual, the status quo, is that it gives no one the opportunity for growth.

The time will come when change will be an imperative. The leader, therefore, has to discern and anticipate change. Otherwise, change will come as an element of surprise, throwing the leader into a storm of defensive tactics, and everyone else for that matter. Leaders caught in this situation find themselves fighting the forces of nature, ultimately sailing to wherever the wind takes them. Best is for the leader to discern when change is necessary, set the right conditions for success, and lead the ship and its occupants, with determination, to safe waters.

What happens when you know change must happen? When change must occur, we know courageous leadership will be necessary, and that means you, as the leader, will have to inject discomfort into relationships, disturb the status quo, and you, most likely, will face isolation (many will oppose you). It's no wonder why going back to the boat and sailing to the known land of status quo is so easy and comforting.

There, everyone can continue to operate under a self-deceiving safety net. But what would happen if you, as a leader, and your team knew there was no going back? The answer is that when you have no option but to achieve your conquest, you have to (and you will) find a way.

The second lesson we can draw is closely related to the first. Once you have decided that you have reached the point of no return, something happens within you. An unexplainable transformation occurs in your chemistry and produces determination. Your power becomes focused. Your convictions become clearer. Your resolve becomes stronger. This is the reason why you can then conquer the unimaginable and can win battles even when you're outnumbered six to one.

If there are conquests on the horizon, don't wait. Stop giving yourself or your team the choice to go back to life as usual—followers dislike leaders who can't make up their minds. Give yourself but one choice: victory in your conquest! If you become determined and give no one any other choice, then you will become a leader.

The Conformist

Leadership means finding new direction, not simply putting yourself at the front of the herd that's heading toward the cliff.

~William Deresiewicz, address to West Point Academy, October 2009

Ore than 1,800 years ago, a man named Claudius Ptolemy lived in the city of Alexandria, in the Roman province of Egypt during the second century. Tales say he had a vision that led him to observe the skies, the moon, and the stars.

As he spent time in solitude observing the movement of the stars and the moon, he came to see that the moon and the planets moved in complex predictable patterns, with the earth being the center of that entire magnificent universe. He annotated all of his observations in a book called the *Almagest*.[21] For nearly 1,500 years, this book became the thesis on all aspects of mathematical astronomy, solar, lunar, and planetary theory.

More than a thousand years later, another man by the name of Nicolaus Copernicus also developed a keen interest in astronomy. He also read the *Almagest* and compared his observations with those of Ptolemy.

---

[21] "Greek Mathematics and Its Modern Heirs: Classical Roots of the Scientific Revolution," Library of Congress, http://www.ibiblio.org/expo/vatican.exhibit/exhibit/d-mathematics/Greek_math2.html.

Copernicus discovered errors in some of Ptolemy's calculations.

"No, the earth is not the center of the universe," he began to believe. He doubted himself, and in his research, he discovered he was not the only one who thought this way. An ancient writer and Greek astronomer had also suggested the earth moved around the sun and not the other way around.

Copernicus wrote his observations in a book called *On the Revolutions of the Heavenly Spheres*. His ideas were marginalized, and his book was made prohibited reading for decades.[22]

Nearly two hundred years later came Galileo Galilei with the same inquisitive mind. He began to experiment, observe, and compare his observations of the stars with that of others. He also discovered Copernicus's book. In secret, he read and made his own observations, spending a long time trying to figure out how things worked. One day, through the lens of a

---

[22] S. Wise Bauer and Jeff West, "The New Universe," *The Story of the World: The Middle Ages, from the Fall of Rome to the Rise of the Renaissance*, 2nd rev. ed., vol. 2 (Charles City, VA: Peace Hill, 2007), 334–341.

telescope, he made some new discoveries (the moon was not flat, Jupiter had revolving moons, Venus had phases just like the moon) and realized Copernicus was right.[23]

The rest, as we know, is history. We know how Galileo's discovery of the truth and subsequent writings ended in his isolation and punishment. But the truth persisted, and now we revere him as the one who laid the foundation for modern physics and astronomy.

We remember studying those examples in the early years of school. But I believe we don't spend much time thinking about what those examples mean to us today, especially as leaders (or conformists?).

The earlier stories highlight several key points in a leader's leadership journey. First, traditional thinking and legacy beliefs are not inescapable and unmovable. I mean, they are not irrefutable laws. They're almost always the starting point of discoveries and should be treated that way.

If you, as a leader, see traditional thinking, for example, as more than just the starting point for

---

[23] "Galileo," Bio, A&E Television Networks, August 16, 2015, http://www.biography.com/people/galileo-9305220.

discoveries, you will never bridge the gap between the past and the future. You will risk going a thousand years without any real progress. In other words, you will forfeit the future of the people and organizations you're charged with leading.

A second key point worth discussing is that of becoming a conformist. Copernicus's and Galileo's stories speak to how crucial it is for a leader to avoid conformism. They speak to the effects of being inquisitive, having independent thought, and having courage. Can you, in your leadership journey, ask the same questions Copernicus and Galileo asked? Why do things work? Is there a better way? Can we get better results? If you want to be a real leader, you need to explore and push those boundaries.

I know many people who want to be the leader at the helm. They would do anything to hold the distinguished position, but do nothing to rock the boat and disturb their chances to be the leader at the helm. Therefore, they become conformists. They'd rather stay quiet and let their organizations do business as usual than disrupt the organization to make it resilient in order to survive the challenges of new and emerging realities.

Break away from being a conformist. Be original in your thinking (think for yourself) but networked in your thinking approach. Individualized thinking that is networked builds the complete picture. In other words, when I say don't be a conformist, I mean, be original in your thinking but network your thinking with those of others so you, as the leader, can harness the collective creativity and ingenuity of the team and build something that is new, dynamic, and adaptable.

We all have a piece of the answer; no one person holds the entire answer. That's because there can be no monopoly of the truth. The truth is free; it belongs to all, but it needs to be discovered, and that takes leadership effort.

Here, now, you have to make a decision. You can decide to keep things going (conform to the existent blueprint doing good work, of course, but not adding value to your or others' existence), or you can begin to challenge conventional thinking and give birth to a world of opportunities.

Spend time thinking about how things work. Spend time developing your own thoughts. Then act accordingly. Network your mind with the minds of your team. If you can do this, then you will become the leader!

José A. LugoSantiago

Becoming Average or Excellent

Encourage all your virtuous dispositions, and exercise them whenever an opportunity arises; being assured that they will gain strength by exercise, as a limb of the body does, and that exercise will make them habitual.

~Thomas Jefferson

Success feels good, but once you've achieved the goal you purposefully marked for yourself, you will enter a very dangerous zone. That zone is quicksand. Some people don't recognize it until it is too late: when they become the *Average.*

I've seen it, and this is how the process starts. You will begin to admire past successes. You may even fall in love with what you've accomplished and feel mighty. Why not? You're a grandiose leader! No one can touch you now because you own the world.

You will begin a series of denials. Good counsel will come to you, but you will forsake it. Of course, you've achieved great feats in life's battle. You've used your sword like no other. How could someone dare try to teach you how to better use the sword? Hasn't everyone heard the tales of your great feats and seen the magnificent castles you've built?

Slowly, you abandon the drills that were rituals in preparing you for the conquests. Your sword was once sharp; it now begins to get rusty. You've forgotten how to sharpen your sword. You've also spent more than a considerate amount of time admiring the past. Now intoxicated and hypnotized by the past, you can't move too far.

If you don't turn around, you will be destined to perish in every battle and become the Average. Here are four signs that you're becoming the Average:

1. You begin to lack humility. Let me point out first that lacking assertiveness is not a quality of being humble. No, that would be wrong. Humility is courage and conviction. What I mean by lacking humility is that you begin to display the superhero and spotlight-hugger syndrome (to impress upon others that because of you, all things happen). It takes a strong person to be humble. Humility is knowing you have strength, but being willing to share that strength (and build strength in others) to make others stronger.

> People who look down on other people don't end up being looked up to.
>
> ~Robert Half

2. You don't pause to reflect. What made you successful in the past? I don't believe it was pure looks and eloquence. We all could bet it was a combination of

good leadership (intelligence and courage), preparation, opportunity, and having the right people with you. (No, I did not type the last sentence in error: without the right people, you will never achieve full success.) As I type these words, I know these three factors are simplified. There are knowns and unknowns in every success. Pause and reflect.

3. You begin to lack courtesies. One of the most notable characteristics of the Average is lack of courtesy. The Average can't produce courtesy. He or she feels entitled to it. When you feel entitled, you become like a spoiled child: you can't say thank you. Neither will you be able to say sorry. Or say no or yes with a smile. Everyone acts out the abundance of his or her heart. An empty heart will produce emptiness. The Average is also rude and feels justified in his or her behavior.

4. You'll begin to set aside high standards. The Average is pleased with the status quo, and doesn't concern himself or herself with the conduct of others. This means that your conduct will begin to lack a code of ethics, a lack of caring for becoming a better human, and you will not make corrections to others when they depart from acceptable norms.

> The task of leadership is not to put greatness into people, but to elicit it, for the greatness is there already.
>
> ~John Buchan

Perhaps success is the culprit of becoming the Average. Or perhaps it is the failure to recognize that one's success is linked to the actions that are necessary for the formation of a more perfect person: the *Excellent*.

The Excellent contrasts the Average by volumes. First, the Excellent is humble and disciplined. Humble in the sense that he or she knows but needs not to impress others. Disciplined in the sense that the Excellent engages in daily rituals in order to master what he or she already can do right (the sword is always sharp), never satisfied with just being good.

The Excellent carries within a great-full attitude, so courtesies come spontaneously. Therefore, the Excellent's attitude creates an atmosphere of respect and cheerfulness.

The Excellent sets personal high standards and brings out the best in others. Therefore, the Excellent cares and helps others discover what they themselves can't yet see.

If you've achieved success, don't be intoxicated by it. Avoid turning into the Average by keeping your sword sharp and seeking to become the Excellent. If you can do that, then you'll be a leader.

The Pyramids, the Cubit, and You

Until the 19th Century, Khufu's Great Pyramid [of Giza] was the tallest building in the world. It was built in around 2550 B.C. and is made of over 2 million blocks of limestone that were queried nearby. Its proportions are perfectly symmetrical.[24]

---

[24] J. Bingham and E. London, "The Pyramids of Giza," *The Usborne Internet-Linked Encyclopedia of the Ancient World* (London: Usborne, 2002), 104.

Many of us have read about the legends of ancient Egypt. Movies have even been made about it, inspired by the many stories, man's imagination about what could have happened in those days, and how life could have been during ancient times.

It's almost incomprehensible to understand the full science behind how those structures survived the test of time. (Even scientists wonder about that!) But I think I have a foundational piece of the puzzle that answers the incomprehensible enigma.

Centered between the right and left edges of my office desk, I have a hand-carved replica of a unit of measurement called *cubit*.

Upon my departure from Ramstein Air Base, Germany, my Airmen in the Precision Measurement Equipment Laboratory (PMEL[25]) carved a wooden cubit, similar to the one you will see in the following picture, and presented it to me to remind me never to forget

---

[25] The PMEL is part of the Air Force Metrology and Calibration Program. That team's mission is to preserve accurate and precise measurement standards for all air force measurement and weapon systems.

where I came from. The point was to remind me, in my subsequent leadership journey, about the importance of living up to a standard and preserving it!

The Airman making the presentation back then spoke about how the cubit was used in ancient Egypt to build the pyramids. Dr. James Turner, former director of the National Institute of Standards and Technology,[26] gives us a glimpse into the story. It's a true story, dating back more than five thousand years.

The ancient Egyptians were among the first to understand the importance of accurate measurement standards. The most famous? The Egyptian cubit. Based on the length of the pharaoh's forearm and hand, the cubit made possible many of those ancient magnificent structures you see today. But how?

---

[26] J. Turner, "First Arab Conference on Calibration and Measurement," November 6, 2007, http://www.nist.gov/director/speeches/turner_110607.cfm.

A master cubit made out of granite was created. Working copies made out of wood were also created to the exact dimensions and specification of the granite cubit. At each full moon, craftsmen would compare the wood cubits with the master granite cubit to ensure precise accuracy. Failing to do so was punished by death.

That system of strict comparison (and adjustments when needed), made possible accuracies of 0.05 percent over distances of 230 meters. The system also made sure that each stone was perfectly cut and perfectly aligned to its correct place in the pyramid. The result? Inexplicable accuracy and structures that would dare to win the test of time.

Thinking back to the pyramids, I ask myself how long those pyramids would have lasted if no one cared about the standard. I even wonder if those pyramids would have looked like pyramids.

I think about the story of the pyramids and the cubit often, especially when someone's expectation is for me, as a leader, to compromise with wrong. I specifically think about the cubit when another person gets mad because I stayed true to my convictions and did not compromise with standards. I wonder about the world this person with skewed expectations envisions for my organization or me.

I also think about the cubit when I see good people who wrongly compare themselves with others who are clearly not made out of granite. Those people become lousy leaders and followers. That's because comparing oneself to others who are not made out of granite is to assume the danger of assimilating a hollow leadership character, becoming just like them—mediocre leaders whose only concern is their own reputation for personal greatness rather than setting people and organizations up for future success.

My leadership experience and observations of life have taught me many lessons. One of them is that real leaders build lasting success in people and organizations when they care and insist on meeting performance standards. Jim Collins also noted this observation in his famous research of 28 companies who sustained unparalleled performance over a 15-year period.[27] Collins research pointed that those companies

---

[27] J. Collins, *Good to Great: Why Some Companies Make the Leap and Others Don't* (New York: HarperCollins, 2001), 25-30.

had leaders at the helm who were absolutely determined to produce results. Those were leaders who would settle for nothing less than building a great company rather than their own personal fame, enabling the company to sustain growth past their tenures in office.

Another important lesson is that leaders become magnificent structures themselves when they become closer and closer to the granite's lines and specifications. These leaders gain wisdom, knowledge, expertise, and sound judgment because they demand excellence of themselves. The by-product of that excellence is referent power, an attraction of the follower to the leader. These leaders become the real-deal, the tools of choice. And when the master craftsman puts those leaders to the test, the precision of their work and leadership becomes the admiration of many.

In other words, set standards of excellence in behavior, in moral courage, and in work performance; live up to them. Find the granite cubit and compare yourself to it. Be ready to be the master craftsman's most precious and sharpest tool. If you can do that, you'll be a great leader, and your legacy will live for thousands of years!

Keep It Simple

Who said "simple is better"? You may have heard the popular maxim or a variation of it, for example, "keep it simple." Perhaps every leader should repeat and live by that old maxim. In leading people and organizations, that's one of the most important laws of effectiveness. The dilemma is that although we've heard of the maxim, our actions don't always show we're convinced about its truth. We have made a habit of taking the simple and making it complex.

We complain, but we have come to love the feeling of complexities, of being busy, wanting to do it all. What a great rush is to live at high speed, to deal with myriad issues, to think we've become skilled at the art of handling it all! Can it be possible to juggle myriad matters, be everywhere at all times, and still achieve revere detail in our work without bearing the negative consequences? The research says that's not possible—more on that later.

Making the problem even bigger, a prevalent culture exist today that rewards the so-called multitasking. This culture is alive and well, and it leads to self-deception. We have come to believe that multitasking—fast, now, complex, lots—is the way of the rich, the way to a better life, and the way to feel accomplished. Managers in workplaces, for example, look favorably to those who appear to live the multitasking lifestyle; in the marketplace, it's a sought-after skill in prospective employees.[28] Multitaskers are "valued" employees because it appears they can do it all. But have we stopped to think about what this is doing to us? It's an insatiable addiction. We subscribe to multiple magazines, newspapers, uncountable news channels, but we're still hungry. We download the latest apps on our phones and tablets to help us crunch and gather innumerable sources of information to feel connected, but we're still hungry, wondering for more. That's a problem. Did you know scientists have estimated that one weekday edition of the *New York Times* contains more information than the average person in seventeenth-century England would be exposed to in his or her lifetime?[29] Still, that's not enough.

> Everybody gets so much information all day long that they lose their common sense.
>
> ~Gertrude Stein, American novelist and poet

---

[28] Appelbaum, Steven H., Adam Marchionni, and Arturo Fernandez. "The Multi-Tasking Paradox: Perceptions, Problems and Strategies." *Management Decision* 46, no. 9 (2008): 1313-1325.
[29] D. Shenk, "Data Smog: Surviving the Information Glut," *The New York Times*, retrieved December 6, 2014, http://www.nytimes.com/books/first/s/shenk-data.html.

So what does this information-hungry, multilevel, and multitasking lifestyle produce? A lifestyle that is adapted to multitasking and being information-hungry produces people who lack attention span and the ability to think. This in turn produces people who are fascinated by complications. Trying to satisfy an urge to know it all, they become weak at sensing and analyzing; hence, they become constantly distracted and unable to organize thoughts.

The research conclusions about the effects of multitasking on cognitive ability and performance are insightful. A group of researchers at Stanford University in 2009 set out to study the cognitive skills of multitaskers.[30] They divided the subjects into light and heavy multitaskers. The research discovered that heavy multitaskers became worse at distinguishing between relevant and irrelevant information. This was not the case with light multitaskers, who were unaffected by distractors and were far more able to filter out the unimportant than the heavy multitaskers could.

---

[30] E. Ophir et al., "Cognitive Control in Media Multitaskers," *Proceedings of the National Academy of Sciences of the United States of America, 106*, no. 37 (2009): 15583–15587.

Another point highlighted by this research was the effects of multitasking on cognitive recalling of facts (memory). Heavy and light multitasker subjects approached information differently. Light multitaskers had a greater tendency for focus, and therefore, a top-down approach to information gathering and processing, whereas heavy multitaskers used a bottom-up approach. Consequently, heavy multitaskers biased toward an "exploratory, rather than exploitative, information processing." This phenomenon affected how both sets of subjects stored and recalled information. In short, heavy multitaskers had more difficulty filing and recalling information.

Given the insights of this research, can you imagine the costly implications to organizations? Leaders in organizations are paid to think through complex problems, analyze pertinent information, and build courses of action that translate into promising ventures. However, if a leader can't distinguish between what is and is not relevant, how can he or she really lead? More than likely, leadership will not be effective because the analytical capacities of the leader to make critical decisions are already been affected; in the end, the effects will cost organizations millions, and these organizations will not even know it.

Then, what can leaders do? Many of us in high executive leadership positions are addicted to information and addicted to the rush of doing multiple things at once. It's a craving that can get us distracted a whole day without achieving any real, positive results. We need to break away from it. We need to change our beliefs and the organizational culture.

Here are a few words of advice. Keep what you're doing simple! If you've subscribed to three newspapers, cut those subscriptions to one. If you think that's not going to give you enough of what you need, then identify in your workplace those people of good character who seem to know it all and ask them about daily events or the latest news they've heard. This action not only will free your personal time, but also will help you develop the art of conversation and will help you cultivate relationships with your team members.

If you have your e-mail open all the time while you work on your computer, consider turning it off. Check your e-mail at specific blocks of time during the day. (Better is to check e-mail at, for example, 8:00 a.m., noon, and 4:00 p.m. than checking it every time an e-mail pops up. The latter will kill your productivity and creativity.) Give your focus to e-mail for no more than thirty minutes at a time.

Instead of multitasking, do time management. Studies have shown that time management has been superior to multitasking.[31] The distinction here is the allocation of individual focused time to diverse tasks. If you have to do several things concurrently (and I'm sure you must), then allocate and distribute the time for the activities, rather than trying to switch from one activity to another.

Lastly, if you must multitask regularly and heavily, consider delegating tasks. This action will help you identify and grow talent in your organization. You may also consider outsourcing work that is not aligned with core business processes in your organization. These actions will further develop your leadership skills.

---

[31] Otto, Susannah C., Katie R. Wahl, Christophe C. Lefort, and Wyatt H. P. Frei. "Exploring the Impact of Multitasking in the Workplace." *Journal of Business Studies Quarterly* 3, no. 4 (06, 2012): 154-162.

In short, keep it simple, stay focused, and free yourself from excess multitasking. Your mind will be sharper and your decision-making more effective. If you can do this, then you'll be the leader we want to follow.

Snow Angels

People want to be creatively satisfied, and having fun is such an important part of that.

~John Lasseter, creative advisor to Walt Disney
Imagineering

The winter of 2014 in Washington, DC, was unforgettable. Snow? Plenty! I had not seen that much snow in several years. Many in the DC area claimed the 2014 winter to be one of the coldest they've had in years. Although cold, I remember the cold was never an excuse to go out and make the best out of it. I remember...

While working an important project in my office, my executive assistant knocked insistently on the door and told me, "Chief, the general wants to speak with you quickly."

Judging from the tone in his voice, the matter was important and urgent, so I stopped what I was doing and proceeded to the general's office.

The general looked at me and said, "Chief, get as many people from the headquarters as possible. We're going outside to do snow angels."

After hearing those words, I paused for a moment to think about what I'd just heard. Snow angels? Maybe this was some kind of code word for an operation or project that I was not aware of. (In the military, we used code all the time, so surely this meant something else. Maybe "angels" meant warriors, and "snow" was the acronym for the operation.)

Anyway, I decided to ask what I was sure to be a series of stupid questions. "General, did you say 'snow angels'?"

"Yes, Chief. That's what I said." The general replied.

Confused, I looked outside, pointed at the window where I could see the snow from, and asked, "Do you mean outside, in the snow, making angels?"

The general was looking seriously at the computer screen, acting fast to shut down the computer, and then surveying the office quickly to locate a hat. I knew then the general was serious.

I said, "I got this, General." I went out of the office and told the first sergeant and directors to assemble as many people as we could because we were going outside to make snow angels. Every time I told a troop (NCO, civilian, or senior officer), they would look at me and ask, "Did you say 'snow angels'?"

"Yes," I replied, "General's orders." So we all went outside with our jackets on, our hats and gloves and lined up. I have to admit, we were a little puzzled.

But at the general's command, we laid on the snow and began to do jumping jack motions to form snow angels (the general included).

Soon, one could hear everyone's laughter. Several unit members took out their phones and cameras and began taking pictures of that moment. Others began to play with snowballs. Those were some fun twenty minutes!

As everyone returned to the building, I continued to hear the laughter and renewed energy in unit members. Surely those members, like me, would remember that moment for years to come.

That moment taught me several things. Among them, the leader has to make the best out of a situation. Sometimes we, as leaders, wait for the perfect situation to do something. Delaying action is not always the best strategy.

The best strategy is the one that seizes the moment. One cannot wait until tomorrow to make a situation ideal. If the situation is not ideal, make it so.

Hoping for a better or ideal day tomorrow? Why do that when you have today? As a leader, make the best out of your people's day, and yours, today. Be bold and do something fun that breaks the monotony of a workday. Get everyone involved.

As a leader, don't miss an opportunity to remind everyone that any day can be a good day. You just have to think differently about your circumstances. So get out of the office, rally your people, get outside, and have some fun!

If you can do this, you will inject a positive flow of energy in the workplace, your people will learn to make the best out of every situation, and you will gain the trust to become the leader they want to follow!

José A. LugoSantiago

III. ACHIEVING AUTHENTICITY

Fusing the Strong Heart and the Clever Mind

The heart and the mind must work harmoniously, feeding each other the right elements at the right time to turn an ordinary person into the ultimate and authentic leader.

In the heart, there is strength, energy, and power. In the mind, there is vision and calculation of what is possible. Between the heart and the mind exists the instinct to know what's right and what's not, the chemistry to regulate energy for action and inaction, and the wisdom to produce determination and endurance until one is victorious.

This section combines those elements of the heart and mind to produce an effect. The effect is authentic (real) leadership that demonstrates self-control and wisdom, influence over others, trust in relationships, care for the development of others, and action that is purposeful. Let's put the heart and mind together.

Power Intoxicates

Power tends to corrupt, and absolute power corrupts absolutely.

~Sir John Dalberg-Acton

O n my leadership journey, I have met and advised leaders who, although seemingly good natured at one time, over time began thinking more of themselves than of others. They once had the heart and mind of a leader, but they were no longer the leaders we would like to follow. The longer they were in a leadership position and the higher they climbed the career ladder, the more they believed in their own superiority.

Sir Dalberg-Acton, in his words, makes a powerful observation that may explain the phenomenon. He notes that innate in the human race exists the tendency to be intoxicated by power. Power is like good wine. Once you've had a taste of it, you want to have more of it, but too much of it will impair you. There lies the danger, according to Sir Dalberg-Acton.

Think about this for a second. You've worked hard, and finally, you're at the helm. You're the boss! Now in the leadership role, you begin to enjoy yourself despite the stressors that might come daily. You begin to be admired by others, your orders are being followed, and your ideas are so marvelous they begin to materialize as you speak. You're the one, the chosen one!

If you don't think about what you may be experiencing, and you let the illusions control you, your view of reality will become distorted, and that will cloud your judgment. That's called intoxication. It happens to many great people, and unfortunately, they turn into spoiled children: uncontrollable and entitled.

> Three-star general "failed to treat his subordinates with dignity and respect" when he unleashed a tirade loaded with f-bombs during a 2014 briefing.
>
> ~Headline on local newspaper

The consequences of having leaders who are intoxicated by power is disastrous for people and organizations. Headlines in newspapers, like the one you just read, are examples of the behavior leaders begin to exhibit when intoxicated by power. Those leaders become detached and insensitive to their environment. Their sense of entitlement compels them to treat others as pawns instead of partners. Those leaders see organizations as hierarchical, with the follower holding the duty to comply and execute orders. Scholars call this the normative duty to obey,[32] where leaders see themselves as the legitimate agents of an organization and the others must occupy the role of subordinates.

---

[32] B. E. Ashforth and V. Anand, "The Normalization of Corruption in Organizations," *Research in Organizational Behavior: An Annual Series of Analytical Essays and Critical Reviews*, vol. 25 (2003): 1–52.

Examples also abound in other areas of society. In business, we saw examples like the Enron scandal. Corporate executives felt empowered to act unethically, rationalizing their wrong doings, stealing millions. Those corporate executives created a culture where leaders pursued and celebrated personal gain, while suppressing those who dissented.[33] Politics is not immune either. All of us, at one point or another, have heard of politicians who have entered in unlawful practices to satisfy personal interests or to get ahead. We hear, for example, about politicians engaging in vote trading in exchange for campaign contributions. In turn, those politicians have avoided making tough decisions for fear of losing campaign contributors.[34] The results of this power intoxication, as you can deduct, are the creation of workplace environments where no one trusts or respects each other, and the rapid degradation and collapse of organizations.

---

[33] C. Pearce et al., "The Roles of Vertical and Shared Leadership in the Enactment of Executive Corruption: Implications for Research and Practice," *The Leadership Quarterly* 19, no. 3 (2008): 353–359.

[34] L. Drutman, "A New Theory of Corporate Lobbying," *The Business of America is Lobbying: How Corporate America Became Politicized and Politics Became More Corporate* (New York: Oxford University Press, 2015), 20.

Are those leaders who became intoxicated bad people? Although some may argue for exceptions, I really don't think so. Those were devoted leaders, smart, and well liked because of who they were as sincere and caring people. Over time, they began doing things that were not right, and on that journey, they lacked followers who were courageous enough to give them needed counsel. Moreover, the leader also failed to stop and think about the real reason he was given privileges commensurate with his or her position.

Maybe I am trying to warn you. No one wants leaders who are intoxicated by power, but this is a danger inherit in your human nature, accelerated by the glamour of being in a leadership position. How will you stay in check?

Here's some simple advice—if you heed it, you will be impactful and memorable in a very positive way. First, understand why you were put in the position you're in. A purpose-driven life is a force that will keep your mind and heart from avoiding unworthy things that lead to your own self-destruction.

Second, be determined in your purpose but flexible in your approach. Know the thing you must accomplish, but be a tactician about how you get it. When you're considering courses of action, many times you will see options A and B clearly. Go for a third alternative. And if you can see options A, B, and C, ask, "Is there an option D?" Or ask, "Can the combination of those options be a more suitable approach?"

Third, don't do all the thinking. You cannot be the only one thinking in your organization, nor can you be the only one with good ideas. Surround yourself with independent thinkers, people who are of good character and will not be afraid to tell you when you're off track. Those people will be your greatest assets, whether you like them or not.

Fourth, delegate as much as you can. Give power (and accountability) to those you delegate so they can carry out their duties and empower their teams to be creative. Make sure they know the credit will be all theirs. Remember, you don't need the credit.

Lastly, but of the utmost importance, treat others as you would a superior. When I first typed this line, I started with, "Treat others with respect; apologize sincerely when you're wrong." However, this is so overused; leaders don't understand it, especially seasoned leaders. So here, I used "treat others as you would a superior." This puts things into another perspective. Let me give you some quick examples:

Starting e-mails with "Yeah, give it to me ASAP!" Would you write to a superior in the same way?

Going to a meeting moody and then behaving like everyone must put up with your temper. Imagine that there were two of your superiors in the room. Would you behave toward them in the same way?

Meeting a junior team member and getting to the bottom-line, ignoring common courtesies. Would you do that to a superior? You would probably start with a "Good morning, sir or ma'am" before you jump right into the business.

> Don't let your ego get too close to your position, so that if your position gets shot down, your ego doesn't go with it.
>
> ~Colin Powell

As many would say, the little things are the things that matter, but in avoiding intoxication, there's more to think about. Avoiding intoxication means that you care for yourself and others. It means that you use power rightfully and with reason, understanding why the organization (or the people) gave it to you. It also means you respect yourself and others, and you demonstrate that in your daily deportment.

If you can avoid being intoxicated, you will become the leader we long for, the one we want to follow.

Politics! You'll Be Tempted

One winter a Farmer found a Snake stiff and frozen with cold. He had compassion on it, and taking it up, placed it in his bosom. The Snake was quickly revived by the warmth, and resuming its natural instincts, bit its benefactor, inflicting on him a mortal wound. "Oh," cried the Farmer with his last breath, "I am rightly served for pitying a scoundrel."

~Aesop's The Farmer and the Snake

Many aspiring and even some senior leaders see politics just as in Aesop's fable. Perhaps, at one point in their careers they met someone who they trusted, helped, and confided with their tricks of the trade, only to later find out that person was using them for personal interest, mainly to get ahead. They felt as if bitten by the snake, despite their demonstrated good will.

When leaders experience the situation I just described, they adopt, in general terms, one of three schools of thought:

1. Politics! It's a dirty business; I don't get involved. Let politicians do whatever they do, as long as they leave me alone. (*Ignore it*)

2. Politics! Since I want to get ahead, I'll play the game. Sorry, dude; it's not personal. It's just the way business goes. (*All about me*)

3. Politics! Because I care about people and their future, I'll need to do my part and shape the outcomes that affect them. (*Involved-aware*)

An authentic leader will not act irresponsibly by ignoring the environment. He or she would not subscribe to an "ignore it" school of thought and let things just happen. Nor will he or she join the "all about me" school of thought because that doesn't align with the leader's nature (self-preservation is not the driving intrinsic motivator).

In whatever leadership environment you find yourself in, there is always a temptation to get in it thinking about Aesop's fable. Don't! Otherwise, you'll be tempted to play politics to appease people, gain social credit, or belong to a tribe, playing it safe because there may be snakes waiting for the opportune moment to bite. Therein lies the danger.

You need to change how you feel and think about the political environment. Find your true self and right mind-set so you can navigate through the perilous trails and shape outcomes that affect people now and in the future. You must shape those outcomes without compromising yourself. Will that feel, at times, like an impossible task? Sure! But history has plenty of examples of heroes who were able to do just that.

> If the American people don't love me, their
> descendants will.
>
> ~Lyndon B. Johnson

A master at storytelling and a master influencer, President Lyndon B. Johnson is one of those examples. He found his true purpose, a desire to fight social injustice and poverty in the United States, and using his passion and intellect, he moved to change the future of a nation through monumental legislative feats. In today's era when it's a milestone for a US president to influence Congress and convert talk into law (to enact three or four proposals), President Johnson was able to submit (and Congress enacted) more than one hundred major proposals in each of the eighty-ninth and ninetieth Congresses.[35] At the end of his administration, there were over three hundred major laws passed under his leadership.[36]

---

[35] J. Califano Jr., "Seeing Is Believing—The Enduring Legacy of Lyndon Johnson," the keynote address by Joseph A. Califano Jr. at the Centennial Celebration for President Lyndon Baines Johnson, May 19, 2008.

[36] H. Middleton, "LBJ: Still Casting a Long Shadow," *Prologue* (the US National Archives and Records Administration, Washington, DC), vol. 40, no 2 (Summer 2008).

His incessant quest to change the present and shape the future secured passage of the landmark Civil Rights Act of 1964, Voting Rights Act of 1965, Social Security Amendments Act (Medicare) of 1965, Higher Education Act of 1965, and Immigration and Naturalization Act of 1965.[37] We still benefit and feel the positive effects of his legacy. Forty-three years later, for example, (in 2008) the nation elected an African American as president for the first time in its history, another positive effect of President Johnson's legacy.

Imagine if President Johnson would have subscribed to an "ignore it" school of thought? The United States would be very different now. The point is that in your leadership journey, you will face tough decisions. Instead of playing politics, or ignoring the political climate, decide to get involved and work incessantly to positively shape the outcomes for those you're charged with leading. Make their lives better.

---

[37] H.R.3290—114th Congress (2015–2016): To award a Congressional Gold Medal to Lyndon Baines Johnson, the 36th President of the United States whose visionary leadership secured passage of the landmark Voting Rights Act of 1965, Social Security Amend. Congress of the United States of America.

Here's a word or two of advice, as you get involved. As I mentioned earlier, understand your purpose, but also understand your environment. Let's start with you. Why do you exist in your organization? What kind of decision power do you have? What are your lanes of responsibility? You have to be clear about what you want to accomplish and why. Understanding that something needs to be done is knowledge. But understanding why something needs to be done is power. Do you know what skills you have and what you don't? Now, let's talk about others.

Look at your external environment and ask yourself a few questions. Do you know who you are connected to? Who you know and what doors those people can open for you are important aspects in making your strategic assessments. Who are the major players? Who has decision power? Who are the gatekeepers? Who are they connected to? And what are their agendas?

As you move in that environment, with a good sense of answers to the questions you just read, begin to act according to your values. Whether people love you is irrelevant. You'll catch people's attention when they can tell you have integrity. Therefore, stand clear from gossip, questionable judgements, and a negative attitude. Get to know people, and beware of being reeled into personal arguments or personal opinions that are inconsequential. Better is for you to assume a more organizational stand on issues, so your view can be holistic rather than shortsighted. The practice of thinking from the organizational perspective, since it's much larger, will help you neutralize thinking boxes that your opposition will build just to trap you. Finally, act with good will for all. Even if you find yourself bitten by a snake, you'll garner much more support when people know you're the kind person who's also tough and resilient. And the snake? Don't worry about it. In time, everyone will know who and where it is—and it will be isolated.

Be a leader, an authentic leader for your people and your organization. Shape the outcomes for the now and for the generations to come. If you can do these things, you'll be respected and admired as a leader.

José A. LugoSantiago

Critiquing the Boss Is Critiquing Yourself

It is not the critic who counts, nor the man who points out how the boss stumbled or where the boss could have done better. The credit belongs to whoever can work with that boss to turn him around from his shortcomings. His place shall never be with those cold and timid souls who know neither how to lead nor how to be a good human being.

~Adaptation from Theodore Roosevelt's "Citizenship in a Republic" speech

The easy thing to do is to point out how your boss (or even your predecessor) lacked tactfulness, foresight, courage, patience, or pick any other leadership characteristic from your or other people's assessment of the boss's faults. The difficult, but right, thing to do is to close the door with the boss, give constructive feedback, and help that boss become the leader the organization deserves. That's not easy; only effective, seasoned leaders can master that art.

Working under a good boss who challenges the people and the organization, who at the same time recognizes, and appreciates everyone's small victories is easy. The test of true leadership is working with a difficult, unaware, and sometimes self-centered boss. How do you lead, coach, and mentor that person? Is it good leadership (and good followership) to do your task and lead others to do theirs while passively trying to overcome that person's shortcomings? The answer is no.

Passively going your way is irresponsible. People who assume that operating style display a careless attitude toward the organization and its people. They are not just careless, but they also demonstrate a lack of courage to confront the leader and a lack of intellect to influence the leader and the future of the organization. Assuming a passive attitude is like reducing oneself to a mere pawn (the weakest piece on the chessboard). As the boss makes mistakes, you look the other way and lament to everyone how this person is missing the mark, as if you knew better or could do better. You wait for that person to make another mistake or display a lack of proficiency so you can use the opportunity to correct it and demonstrate to others how smart you can be.

That's awful. I'll tell you why. You are institutionalizing unethical norms of conduct for those in the organization and for those future leaders who will come after you. In other words, those who see your attitude will begin to act in the same manner when they are in your position. Imagine if you get to be in your boss's position. Would you also like that type of passive sabotage from those you lead to go on? I am certain the answer is no.

The other point to consider is the damage to your credibility as a leader. I have seen leaders who begin to criticize their superiors (or predecessors) in meetings with their departments or organizations, ranting about how x or y decision was stupid. Those same leaders then offer how they would have done it better, thinking that those who are listening would see how the leader (or the predecessor) was incompetent and how much smarter the new leader is. Again, this is awful, so don't take part in it. If you do, those listening will know better—never underestimate those who work for you. They will listen to your rants, and then go to others to criticize you (they will go to other informal leaders or even the person you just criticized). Those listening will talk about your lack of character and insecurities. Plainly said, they will display the same attitude toward you (or worse). They will know that, since you lack character, you can't be trusted.

As a leader, you've failed, and you will have to work hard to gain your people's trust. They will want to have peace in their minds that when they experience discord with you, you will not treat them in the same way you treated those who were superior to you.

> To retain those who are present, be loyal to those who are absent.
>
> ~Dr. Stephen R. Covey

Instead of criticizing or waiting passively, do better: adapt and coach. When I look through the life's story of highly successful, respectable leaders (in the public and private sector), adaptation and coaching seem to be the predominant bedrocks in becoming effective leaders. This is important to note because seldom does one have the option to pick the leader. Some of us are appointed to positions of trust under key leaders. Some of us are hired into the organization to work special projects or lead teams under the direction of another team leader. Regardless, one has to be able to adapt to the leader, gain the trust of that leader, and then properly influence and coach that leader for the good of the organization and its people. How can we do that?

In 2012, I had the honor of meeting the Chairman of the Joint Chiefs of Staff, General Martin E. Dempsey. I was part of a senior leader enhancement program, learning about and touring several key national command authorities in the northern part of the Americas. We, as a small group, were to meet with General Dempsey as part of our experience. He spent several hours with us at the Pentagon talking about national military strategy, geopolitical matters, and leadership at a national strategic level. I met him again in 2013 while I was assigned to the National Capital Region in a key leadership position. Both times (but certainly more the second time when I had the opportunity to watch more closely some of the inner affairs of Washington, DC), I thought he was quite the model leader: adapter, influencer, and coach.

Put yourself in this leader's position for a few minutes. As the chairman, he is the senior ranking member of the armed forces of the United States. Although he is the most senior, he does not command the forces per se. By public law, Congress gave that authority to combatant commanders.[38] Still, he has some broad and specific responsibilities to the military services (see the following footnote).[39] He is also the principal military advisor to the President of the United States, the National Security Council, and the secretary

---

[38] H.R. 3622—99th Congress, Goldwater-Nichols Department of Defense Reorganization Act of 1986: "Provides that the operational chain of command for combatant commands shall run from the President to the Secretary of Defense to the commanders of the combatant commands."

[39] H.R. 3622—99th Congress, Goldwater-Nichols Act specifies that the Chairman presides over the Joint Chiefs of Staff, other functions relating to the planning of military manpower, strategy, and readiness capabilities, and reports to the Secretary of Defense concerning recommended changes in the function assignments of the armed forces.

of defense. He also operates under the direction of the secretary of defense. One can only imagine the kind of pressure that exists in a position like his as he deals with the politics of Washington, the culture of each of the military departments, the personalities of presidential appointees and elected officials, the management of two wars, and the entire national security effort.

During his tenure as chairman, General Dempsey served four secretaries of defense. He served under Robert Gates, Leon Panetta, Chuck Hagel, and Ash Carter. He described each as very different from the other.[40] An inexperienced leader in a situation like his could have defaulted to a natural like-or-dislike attitude, meaning he could better work with one but not the other. An inexperienced leader could have also tried to change to make himself well liked. The general elected neither. Instead, he understood his leader and adapted himself to each.

Each of those leaders he worked for had a different executive experience, a different way to interact with the environment, and a different way to

---

[40] J. J. Collins and R. D. Hooker, "From the Chairman: An Interview with Martin E. Dempsey," *Joint Forces Quarterly* (National Defense University), no. 78 (2015): 11–12.

learn and acquire information. For example, he describes Secretary Gates as a voracious reader; the written word informed him. Secretary Panetta learned more through interaction, so every interaction he had with people and his staff informed him and helped shape what he already knew. Secretary Hagel had a great instinct for detail, so the general would choose his words carefully on correspondence, stating that he would write many of the reports himself instead of doing cursory checks of completed staff work, and then sending those reports to Secretary Hagel.

The general's experience shows a lesson that every good leader should embrace. Rather than trying to critique the boss or succumb to a like-or-dislike attitude, try to understand the leader's experiences, environment, and learning style. Then adapt to those factors. Once you connect, because you're able to adapt, you'll be able to influence and coach. Your behavior will also be an example of what great leaders should do. Your actions will increase your credibility, and your behavior (watched by everyone who reports to you) will be modeled across your organization, making those who work for you far more efficient and loyal.

There's no magic formula here, but this discussion is a good one for anyone wanting to become an influencer and leader of leaders. Much of your success will come from knowing in your heart what's right, and then thinking through the environment surrounding your situation, your leader's personality, your own personal style for developing relationships, your level of involvement with the leader, and your sincerity in serving that leader and the organization. If you can adapt, influence, and coach, then you'll be a great leader!

José A. LugoSantiago

The Fountain of Youth

Obsession with what you want can get you exactly what you don't want.

An old Puerto Rican legend talks about an eternal fountain of youth. In the early 1500s, the Taino Indians of the small Caribbean island of Puerto Rico told the story to the Spanish conqueror Juan Ponce de León. Tales of the island say he was troubled deeply by the natives' story.

He couldn't resist the impetus to claim that fountain for himself. He armed his men, prepared his ships, and took off out of beautiful San German, Puerto Rico, determined to find its location on an island by the name of Bimini. After many days of terrible maritime weather conditions, he was forced to make a stop in the north of Cuba. He reoriented his fleet and continued his trip, stopping on an "island" he named Florida. He spent over six months exploring, bathing in every small body of water he could find on his journey, to find nothing resembling what he had imagined. He retuned back to Puerto Rico disillusioned.[41]

I heard Alexander the Great, who conquered most of what was known of the world before he died around 323 BC, also searched for this so-called fountain of youth,[42] but not in the Caribbean, of course! Nevertheless, he went on an expedition in the twelfth

[41] C. Coll y Toste, "La Fuente Magica," *Colección de Leyendas de Puerto Rico* (Spanish Edition) (Puerto Rico eBooks, 2015), Kindle locations 1307–1319.
[42] W. Drye, "Fountain of Youth–Just Wishful Thinking?," *National Geographic*, October 10, 2015.
http://science.nationalgeographic.com/science/archaeology/fountain-of-youth/.

century searching for its magic waters. He risked everything.

These two men had riches and power that surpassed by far their contemporaries and the richest person in the modern world today. And although the impetus to move forward was not solely based on more acquisition of riches, one would think they would have been satisfied with the level of admiration and riches they already had. But none of that was enough.

How much is enough? We all read about these examples and can't help but wonder. What makes men keep on looking and not realize they've been given things that others can only dream of?

> The only thing worse than being blind is having sight but no vision.
>
> ~Author Helen Keller

I believe the reason we keep searching for the fountain of youth is because our obsession blinds us. And this is particularly true of leaders who are obsessed with either winning or achieving personal success.

Why am I writing to you about this? Leaders can become self-absorbed in a world of accomplishing things, in a place where only results are the ultimate bottom line. In securing the wins, leaders furiously seek after what they want, disregarding the very laws of nature: that the flower, for example, is the by-product of having the plant grow in fertile ground, with the right amount of water and sunlight.

Self-absorbed, obsessed leaders walk on quicksand; their behavior does not go unnoticed. In time, the word travels through the halls of the workplace, and everyone begins to pay attention. One can see how the obsessed leader begins to ignore the ideas of employees and wants to fly solo. Or when those good ideas come to the ears of the leader, and somehow get executed into success, the leader reaches for an immediate billboard campaign with signs all over the place that say, "I did it!" In the meantime, one can see how the workplace halls get fill with the murmur of employees who say, "He [the leader] only cares about his promotion."

If you're thinking the preceding paragraph described a leader who's selfish and uncaring, you're incorrect. I just described the real story of a leader who had the best of intentions. To tell you the truth, this was a kind-hearted leader. He just didn't know what was happening to him. This leader was under pressure from his boss, and as a good follower, he wanted to demonstrate how capable he was of delivering (and overdelivering) on time and on budget.

His obsession blinded him. Instead of cultivating relationships, he decided to command. Instead of asking why to get to the root cause of bottlenecks in processes, he became impatient and rude to employees, thinking he had lazy employees. What this person did not know was that teams of employees were putting in vast amounts of work, coordination, and long hours at work every day. This leader was also very smart and intellectual, but instead of using the intellect of the organization's employees, he began to do all of the thinking himself. In short, he had all the good ideas, employees felt they were not valued or listened to, and they began to complain about the terrible work environment.

In desperation and good faith, one employee reached out to the leader's mentor and explained the pain the employees were going through. Once the mentor approached the leader and talked with him, things changed. The leader felt terrible about the situation, and thoroughly apologized to the entire team. This leader did not intend to be this way. His obsession, seeking desperately for the fountain of youth, blinded him to the fact that everything he wanted was within his reach. He just needed to treat his employees with respect, listen and take their suggestions, give credit to those employees who were the core of his business, and celebrate with them the small victories. In essence, he needed to work through his team and pour himself into the service of his people.

Beware of becoming obsessed with success as if searching for the fountain of youth. Remember that success is the by-product of cultivating yourself, your people, and the environment where both you and your people operate. If you can understand and act on this principle, you will become an authentic leader, the one we long to follow.

The Puzzle Pieces

Some of us worked hard to fit in. If you don't remember, pull out your old high school pictures. As you looked at those pictures, you probably thought to yourself, "How could I've done that, wore that, or looked like that? Why didn't someone stop me?" Don't be surprised, but think about the reasons you did what you did.

We may have worn the in-style dress, colored shirts, and so on, because we began to notice we were different but did not realize why; we had to try to fit in.

Being different made us uncomfortable. Some of us learned to deal with that, accepted being different, and in the process, grew stronger. Others didn't. Some of us saw how being different gave us an edge in thinking, motivating people, communicating with others, and even helped us adapt to our environment quickly. Others didn't. Being different also meant that we were not always accepted; we were at times labeled, at other times, we were bypassed for opportunities. It was painful sometimes, but once we began to see what our differences allowed us to do in teams, we rejoiced! Being different is a good thing!

In the history of the world, sameness never made breakthroughs. Galileo was different, and he thought differently about the world around him. He gave us the telescope and the notion that the center of our universe was not the earth but the sun. He made a difference because he accepted that he was different and could think differently. Being different is a good thing.

Accepting being different is a much tougher endeavor. Some people never grow out of their high school years. They carry into adulthood those insecurities and still fight to fit in, even when something inside tells them trying to fit in does not fit right. In the end, those people become lousy leaders, because even as adults, still trying to fit in, they disable any opportunity they could have taken to showcase the power of their uniqueness. As a leader, you need to watch for this, in you and in others. Let me explain my point with an example.

Once I met a leader who was making some unwise decisions. Every one of his other key leaders knew about it, but no one wanted to give this leader the bad news. One day, an incident made me think that it was time to talk with this leader. I knocked on the door, and asked to speak with him about the issue. The leader got mad and yelled to his closest advisor to come into the office. Infuriated and after giving a short explanation, the leader asked his advisor, "Am I seeing this wrong?" His trusted advisor glanced at me (I could see in his eyes the internal conflict), and then replied, "Well, sir, that's the way I see it too!" In that team, there was no difference in opinion, no real diversity, and that was necessary to inform and facilitate strategic level decision-making. Later on, I helped this trusted advisor overcome this weakness.

> If two people agree on everything, one of them is not thinking.
>
> ~John F. Kennedy

The above example painted a leader who disliked and alienated anyone who was different or thought differently. What do you think was the result of that behavior? He ended up with people who were just like him, who were also too scared to warn him, the captain of the ship, about how close the ship was to a collision with an iceberg. No leader in today's complex environment can afford a situation like the one I just described.

My point is simple. In becoming an authentic leader, accept that you will think differently than your boss on issues. (And if you don't, you need to create the difference; from time to time, become the difference.) Be willing to explain to the leader that this difference will be the strength in your partnership. Sometimes we think diversity is about race, gender, or culture, but I propose that is far deeper than that—the greatest benefit of diversity is the amplitude of choices and perspectives it creates.

Another point, closely interwoven with the point above, is that anytime you develop the acceptance and moral strength about being different, you also develop an appreciation and acceptance about the differences that exist in those who work for you. You will value your people much more. That appreciation and acceptance will make you stronger as a leader, and that will make your people connect powerfully as a team.

> Research has suggested that diverse working groups can be more innovative, flexible, and productive; [and] can offer valuable perspectives on important issues.
>
> ~ Jefferson P. Marquis et al., RAND[43]

We are all like pieces of a puzzle: different shapes and different colors. You can't take a puzzle, pieces scattered across the table, lift one piece, and then say, "I don't like the shape of this one, so I'm going to toss it." If you do toss a piece, the puzzle will always be incomplete. Every piece in the puzzle fits somewhere and is a critical component of the final masterpiece.

---

[43] J.P. Marquis et al., *Managing Diversity in Corporate America* (Santa Monica, CA: RAND, 2008), 13.

As a leader and human being, you must appreciate the differences (those you see and those you can't). Aim at surrounding yourself with all sorts of shapes and colors. Don't discard the pieces. They all belong together. All of the pieces in the puzzle make a wonderful picture. If you can learn to appreciate this and act on it, you'll become the leader we all want to follow.

Who's Your MTI?

I've been blessed with many opportunities to lead and observe the impact of my leadership on organizations and the people who labor in them. In the lineup of opportunities and blessings, I count serving in the air force as a military training instructor (MTI) as one of the highlights.[44] Why is that?

This immense responsibility taught me important lessons about leadership. Interestingly, I've

---

[44] In other branches of the armed forces, the title for this duty is also known as drill sergeant or drill instructor. Noncommissioned officers in this position prepare men and women for military duty through their particular branch of military service's indoctrination training or boot camp.

found those lessons have direct correlation to leadership at all levels and all settings, regardless of one's hierarchical position in an organization (military or civilian).

The chief lesson of all is that people and organizational performance starts with you! Let me explain through my experience as an MTI, and then take that experience into the context of performing as a senior leader in an organization.

MTIs work countless hours molding young men and women into future leaders—Airmen! In my years as an MTI, I could spot those MTIs who labored hard, who were outstanding, and those who were average—those who did just enough. And you know how I spotted them? Not by interviewing the MTI but by watching the performance of those Airmen he or she led.

> Don't expect apples from a mango tree. The apple tree will bear apples and the mango tree mangos.
>
> ~Old folk adage

The Airmen they led, for the most part, became replicas of their MTIs. They would hunch if their MTI hunched while standing at the position of attention.[45] They would march tall if their MTI marched tall. When Airmen element leaders would be marching formation elements, the enunciation in the cadence when they were giving commands would emulate that of their MTIs. The sharpest of trainees would come from the sharpest of MTIs. In essence, the fallen apple was never too far from the apple tree.

I remember stopping trainees who were not following proper procedures. After a mentoring moment on the proper procedures, I would ask, "Who's your MTI, trainee?" In many instances, the way the young person behaved and demonstrated (or did not demonstrate) military bearing, customs, and courtesies would give me a good clue as to who the responsible leader was. That's because the sharpest MTIs made sure their trainees were attuned to every detail. The best of them would invest considerable time ensuring their trainees were mentally and physically prepared to

---

[45] This is the ability of the trainee to stand upright, chin up but slightly tucked in, chest up, shoulders square, arms straight down with cupped hands, while displaying military bearing (a sign of total emotional and physical control).

confront any situation and produce the utmost precision in procedure and professionalism in military bearing.

It has been twelve years since I last wore the campaign hat,[46] but the things I used to see back then, I repeatedly see in organizations today. Strong leaders in organizations produce outstanding human capital and sharper, more resilient organizations. Strong leaders are those who dedicate themselves to the people they lead. In turn, they grow talented people who become the strongest asset an organization can have. But strong leaders don't stop there. Those same strong leaders pour themselves into every aspect of their organizations, laboring diligently to improve the work environment and the key processes of organizations.

On my leadership journey today, I meet many people. When I meet people with tremendous drive and excellent preparation, I often ask, "Who's the head of your division?" And the answer does not surprise me. In most instances, those workplaces that thrive, where I also see people thriving, becoming innovative, and producing for the organization, are driven by leaders

---

[46] The campaign hat is also known as the drill sergeant's hat. The hat symbolizes the lineage of the past, the heritage of the army, who adopted it in the early 1900s.

who themselves invest a vast amount of time into their people and the environment where they work.

People are the most important asset an organization has, and strong, real leaders know this well. This is not cliché. But do we really believe it? The problem in many workplaces today is that leaders in organizations treat their employees as if they are expendable. If employees are treated that way, how can we truly say we believe people are our most important asset? You need to believe it and act on this belief.

> Managers account for at least 70 percent of variance in employee engagement scores across business units, Gallup estimates.[47]

Forget about your next job; take care of your people first. All your other prayers will then be answered. Your labor-intensive effort in developing people will be paid back to you in double dividends: in employee trust, loyalty, problem solving, enthusiasm, energy to innovate, and more. In other words, if your

---

[47] R. Beck and J. Harter, "Why Great Managers Are So Rare," *Gallup Business Journal*, March 24, 2014, http://www.gallup.com/businessjournal/167975/why-great-managers-rare.aspx.

people know you're sincere and you're investing in them, they will be sincere and invest back in you too! Think about what I just said.

Think back to a time when you worked for someone who had a stake in your success. How did you respond to that person? I bet you were eager to give whatever the person asked of you, and you were willing to work the long hours for that person. Why? Loyalty is the answer! You developed that loyalty through a mutual helping, sincere relationship. Why would this be any different between you and those who work under your leadership? It's not.

This advice is not for rookie leaders but for leaders who want to achieve authenticity. But more often than not, I find myself reminding so-called seasoned leaders to take and act on this simple advice: take care of your people, and they will take care of you; guide and honor your people, and they will guide and honor you!

What does that mean anyway? It means that your actions demonstrate that you value people for what they can offer the organization now and in years to come. You do that by being zealous about securing training for them. You also must challenge and coach them, promote teamwork, and question the status quo. You must give them a clear framework from where they would make decisions and get the job done. Give them timely, honest feedback when they fall short of meeting expectations. As a leader, you also must listen carefully to what is spoken and not, and you need to remove obstacles that impede growth. And one more thing: you must reward in public those who go beyond mere job descriptions to innovate, get results, and promote ethical behavior in the conduct of business.

My point here is that authentic leaders make an impact on people and organizations because they care. They have the inclination to invest in their people and organizations—doing it beyond the job description— creating a sense of pride and character in the people they lead. It's no wonder the best of employees come from the best leaders, and it's not a wonder employees are so loyal to those they recognize as authentic leaders. Real, authentic leaders leave a mark. Be one!

José A. LugoSantiago

The Big Owl

In the early summer of 2015, we traveled for four days across the United States to relocate to a new home in South Texas. We like our new place. We live among good people who share our same interests, and the neighborhood is quiet. We also have a backyard that is perfect for fellowship with friends and family.

One thing I don't like is the amount of birds we have in our backyard. We like birds, and in other houses we've lived, we've built birdhouses to provide water and food for the birds. But the problem in our new home is the excessive amount of birds coming to the backyard, some even venturing onto the terrace and leaving proof they came to visit (you probably know what I mean).

One day, our community's maintenance man came over to fix the kitchen sink plumbing. He looked at the patio through the kitchen window just above the sink and exclaimed, "Wow, you guys have lots of birds in the backyard!"

"Yes, we do," my wife said. "The problem," she continued, "is that we don't know how to keep them away from the terrace."

The gentleman laughed and said, "Just buy a big owl scarecrow and leave it out there." I was surprised by his comment. Although I was not an initial believer, we went ahead, bought the owl, and put it on the terrace on top of a table.

Guess what? The birds stopped coming. They weren't even in our backyard! I was happy. I cleaned the birds' traces from the floor on the terrace and began to enjoy a clean terrace.

Weeks later, I noticed the birds began to come back, little by little. I even saw traces of bird stuff close to the big owl. I was puzzled, asking myself, what changed? "Here we go again!" I thought. "Why are those birds coming back?"

The gentleman who fixed the sink came over again, this time to fix another issue. He asked, "How's the bird situation going?" I told him the birds were coming back. He asked, "Is the owl moving around? Or is the owl always in the same place?"

"Ah, that's it!" I exclaimed. So I started moving the bird around the terrace, weekly. That solved the problem. I just needed an owl that moved around.

You're probably thinking, "Why in the world are you talking about this owl? What does an owl have to do with our subject of authentic leaders, specifically achieving authenticity?" Perfect questions!

Often, we meet people who want to be recognized as the big owl. They want you to see them as the head chief or big leader in the organization. Many of these people live for the recognition but do very little themselves to earn that reputation. Others get into positions of authority, think they've arrived, and stop moving around.

They forget about their responsibility to continue to sharpen themselves and the organizations they work for. They're just there. Watch out! You don't want to be one of them.

Here's an example of what happens when we get infected with the big owl syndrome. In 1989 the International Basketball Federation eliminated a rule that prohibited NBA players from participating in the Olympics.[48] In 1992 the United States began to take advantage of this opportunity, adding NBA players to their lineup and grabbing the gold medal. Several Olympics and world championships later, the US team remained undefeated (twelve years).[36] They were the dream team. But something happened in 2004.

---

[48] Associate Press, "Federation Rule Change Opens Olympics to N.B.A. Players," *The New York Times*, April 8, 1989, http://www.nytimes.com/1989/04/08/sports/federation-rule-change-opens-olympics-to-nba-players.html.

The United States put together another dream team for the 2004 games, built with a combination of veteran players and rising talent, just the best of the best. In their opening game, a confident team (undefeated and stacked by big names like Tim Duncan, LeBron James, etc.) entered the opening game. They were defeated 92–73 by a team from the small (and I must add, beautiful!) island of Puerto Rico—biggest loss in international basketball history.[49]

The US team then worked some razor-thin margin victories over Australia and Greece. This was a rude awakening for the United States. The team could no longer live thinking its game and big owl reputation was going to assure them victories in the future.

I believe this also can happen (and happens) to organizations and leaders. If we live thinking that success in the past will guarantee success in the future, this very thought could be our Achilles heel, leading us to sure defeat.

---

[49] B. Svrluga, "U.S. Men Slammed by Puerto Rico," *The Washington Post*, August 16, 2004, http://www.washingtonpost.com/wp-dyn/articles/A3480-2004Aug15.html.

> The dogmas of the quite past are inadequate to the stormy present. As our case is new, so we must also think anew, and act anew.
>
> ~Abraham Lincoln

If you're going to be a big owl, you will have to work hard. And once you become the big owl, you'll have to think and work harder! My hope is that if you're a big owl, you move around and make things happen. If you do, then you'll be the leader we won't hesitate to follow.

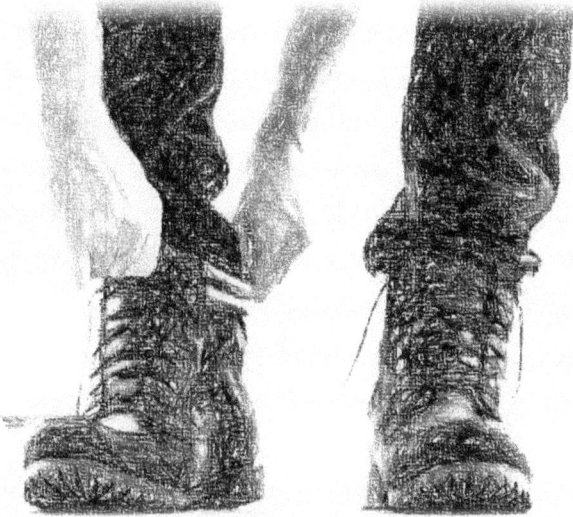

Boots on the Ground: Present for Duty!

Undeniable. The practice of boots on the ground gives a leader the real picture of what's going on. Still, this seems like some kind of extraterrestrial concept to many so-called seasoned leaders. No wonder so many organizations suffer from poor morale, slow growth, and inflexibility to change.

Here is an example of what I'm trying to get across. Have you seen the TV series *Undercover Boss*?

In the TV series, CEOs go undercover into their organizations to find out what really goes on day to day in their businesses.

These CEOs infiltrate their companies as entry-level employees, performing tasks associated with those positions. In the process, the CEOs meet those performing the company's work and learn about the employees' frustrations.

What's most amazing to me is that these high-paid CEOs end up wide-eyed to the problems in their organizations. "I did not know this was breaking...that employees had to work around x, y, or z. I thought the investment was working perfectly!"

> The people in the field are closest to the problem, closest to the situation; therefore, that is where real wisdom is.
>
> ~General Colin Powell

When did we forget this boots on the ground principal? When did the magic of change permeate through organizations neatly, effectively, and without a hiccup? Just like natural law? That just doesn't happen.

If you want to earn the respect of those you lead and truly gain an insight into the business's issues, you have to put boots on the ground at unpredictable times. This natural reflex of putting boots on the ground comes from the leader's realization that leaders are servants to organizations. There is a huge need for this today.

Truly great leaders are present for duty. This means many things. First, present for duty means leaders are visible. They make it a point to visit the areas where the action occurs at unpredictable times. This is what some term going to the battlefield. There is where you seek input on the perceived bottlenecks. And there is where you can fix those bottlenecks. There is where your presence is also needed.

> Presence essentially establishes the leader's seriousness and her or his command of the organization.
>
> ~Rosenbach and Tien[50]

Here's a story to help illustrate the point. During a military expeditionary contingency response exercise,

---

[50] R. L. Taylor and W. E. Rosenbach, "How the West Won: Strategic Leadership in Tal Afar," *Military Leadership in Pursuit of Excellence* (Boulder, CO: Westview Press, 2009).

we deployed to a bare-base region. We needed thousands of sandbags to protect several priority assets. The mission commander for the force gave the force protection order for those key assets, and the order was clear.

As we tracked progress, something did not seem right. The task was taking too long. Additionally, the progress reports seemed contradictory. The reports were telling us that the task was being accomplished as directed and that the adequate number of personnel and resources were on-site. But if everything was going fine, why was the security measure taking so long to accomplish?

I looked at the mission commander and told him, "Give me a radio. I am going down there; I need to see what's going on." I jumped in a vehicle with my wingman, drove, and arrived at the scene.

What I found was incredible. The troops were working hard, but an easy task turned into a very difficult one. Given the condition of the sand, the troops at work now needed special equipment and more manpower. In the meantime, the crew on the ground was making it work in the best way possible. That was a great attitude, but it was not going to get us to the finish line.

The young sergeant in charge was not shy to talk to me about his frustrations. I radioed the mission commander, and the logistics chain was mobilized to give this sergeant what he needed. I thanked this young leader sincerely and spent time with his troops.

It was a very hot day that day, but regardless of the difficulties, the troops were making things happen. Hours later, we declared, "mission accomplished."

Months later, I heard about how much the troops appreciated my trip to their work area and my time afterward chatting with them.

So what's my point? First, be a servant present for duty. Be visible in good and bad times. Make time to go and see those who provide services to you, regardless of who has accountability. Second, go to the "battlefield" and learn about your troops' difficulties. While there, take the time to understand exactly what impedes swift action, and do what you can to remove the obstacles. Honestly, what I'm talking about here is servant leadership; our organizations and our people need it today. Servant leaders place the good of followers ahead of their own. Servant leadership is also about having foresight, having a clear sense of direction, and taking responsibility for the leadership role, and it is about empowering people by serving them.[51] Scholar Robert K. Greenleaf first coined the phrase "servant leader" in the 1970s. If you're not clear about its meaning, I suggest you learn about it; do your own research, and practice its principles. This is no touchy-feely stuff. Servant leadership is tough business.

If you can place boots on the ground, being present for duty with a servant leader attitude, you will build trust, loyalty, and in the end, you will always accomplish much more than barking orders from an ivory tower. Your "troops" will certainly appreciate it. I also can assure you, if you can do this, you will become their leader.

---

[51] P. G. Northouse, "Servant Leadership," *Leadership: Theory and Practice*, (7th Edition), (Thousand Oaks: SAGE, 2016), 226-228.

Final Thoughts

You don't need much to live happily. And just because you've abandon your hopes of becoming a great thinker or scientist, don't give up on attaining freedom, achieving humility, serving others, obeying God.

~Emperor Marcus Aurelius Antoninus, *Meditations*

There we were! It was a Wednesday morning. The theater was crowded with young leaders who were searching for the clues to their future success. This crowd came to us for wisdom. And I was there as part of an invitation from the community who wanted me to speak on my experience as a leader, along with three other panel members.

The young leaders who filled the theater came not because we were old and wise—well, the old was certainly not because of me—of course not! Those leaders came to us because they figured that due to our combined years of experience, we might have something important to say that could help them find the magic link to future success. We gave it our best shot.

They asked many good questions, but one of them asked the most enlightening of questions: "If you could talk to your young you, what advice would you give him or her?" Now, that was a good question!

I thought for a moment about that question. What would I say to young me? What advice would I give him? Where do I start? All of us at the end of our lives aspire to say we lived a life of meaning and purpose. Then, a good start to find the answer to the initial question is to go forward to the day of our observance. As we're looking around and people talk about our life, what will they say? Or better yet, what would we like them to say?

Put yourself in the place I was for a moment. How would you respond? I'm sure you can give yourself lots of advice. Well, I can quickly think of a few pieces of advice, for example, invest in property early, be part of a cause, plant a tree, listen to others, tell someone you love him or her (I hope you do this last one often).

"When things get tough," I would tell my young self, "this too shall pass." I would also tell young me to stay in the present and enjoy the moment and enjoy the people I am with right now. Tomorrow, well, I really don't know if it will come, so I must heed sage counsel, "Do not let the sun go down while you are still angry."[52] In other words, I must try to resolve differences and seek accord with my neighbor.

As a young leader, I would tell young me to meditate about what Marcus Aurelius cited at the beginning of this "Final Thoughts" section. As the philosopher and emperor of Rome put it, you don't need much to be happy. In the end, all of these things, sometimes thought to be the things we need, such as status, cars, and other materialistic things, cannot and will not fill the emptiness of a lonely and sad soul. The things that matter are those that become eternal, such as serving others and making a difference in somebody's

---

[52] Ephesians 4:26. The point here is to resolve differences with others. Otherwise, time will only strengthened the discord.

life, achieving mastery of oneself, and believing in something good.

From one leader (myself) to another (you), if I can leave you with a short lasting thought, it would be this:

My friend, be happy. Learn from your mistakes, and do your best. As you walk along the leadership journey, be the change you want to see in the world, as Mahatma Gandhi said, by nurturing your heart and your mind. Then invest in others and yourself by cultivating meaningful relationships with those who work closest with you; empower them! Only then will your life and legacy as a leader be massively rich. And that's what this book has been all about.

Always motivated,

Lugo

It has been my honor to be your leadership advisor and coach. I would like to hear from you. Send me a note at real_leaders@joselugosantiago.com and let me know how these words inspired and guided you along your journey. Be great!

José A. LugoSantiago

About the Author

———————

José A. Lugo Santiago has over twenty-five years of leadership experience and formal education in several leadership disciplines. The author is a senior executive leadership consultant, manager, trainer, and human capital strategist with the responsibility to oversee, manage, and develop a workforce of thousands. In short, he wakes up and labors every day to develop the engine that makes every endeavor successful: people!

He is also the author of *On the Leadership Journey: 30 Conversations about Leading Yourself and Others*, a fresh perspective that encapsulates our everyday life experience into a transformational leadership mind-set. He is also an avid writer and speaker on the topic of leadership, organizational behavior, and motivation. His blog, *José LugoSantiago--Craft Your Journey! (at* www.joselugosantiago.com), followed by thousands, features a weekly fresh perspective on everyday leadership.

The work in his books and commentaries represent Lugo's boots-on-the-ground framework of leadership study and philosophy. Although tightly woven in timeless leadership tenets, this is not about leadership acquired in the quietness of a classroom.

What you see in Lugo's writing and leadership talks is proven ground in response to questions thousands are asking about leading themselves and others. Regardless of your background—civilian, military, community organizer, or business leader—consider this book your personal leadership coach.

www.ingramcontent.com/pod-product-compliance
Lightning Source LLC
Chambersburg PA
CBHW051825040426
42447CB00006B/381